All I Said Was #*%$

All I Said Was #*%$

STORIES FROM A LIFETIME OF YOUTH MINISTRY

STAN KISTE

RESOURCE *Publications* • Eugene, Oregon

ALL I SAID WAS #*%$
Stories From a Lifetime of Youth Ministry

Copyright © 2022 Stan Kiste. All rights reserved. Except for brief quotations in critical publications or reviews, no part of this book may be reproduced in any manner without prior written permission from the publisher. Write: Permissions, Wipf and Stock Publishers, 199 W. 8th Ave., Suite 3, Eugene, OR 97401.

Resource Publications
An Imprint of Wipf and Stock Publishers
199 W. 8th Ave., Suite 3
Eugene, OR 97401

www.wipfandstock.com

PAPERBACK ISBN: 978-1-6667-3699-1
HARDCOVER ISBN: 978-1-6667-9600-1
EBOOK ISBN: 978-1-6667-9601-8

JANUARY 20, 2022 9:27 AM

To Luanne, an equal partner in this journey every single step of the way. Your purposeful determination to invest in others without recognition is the truest example of a servant's heart. Thank you for your patience, support, and love.

Contents

Acknowledgments | ix

Introduction | 1

Chapter 1	That's Not Ministry	6
Chapter 2	All I Said Was #*&$	9
Chapter 3	A Minty Fresh Buzz	12
Chapter 4	The Gales of October	14
Chapter 5	Speechless	18
Chapter 6	Who Did You Say Is in Charge?	22
Chapter 7	Rising above the Darkness	24
Chapter 8	What This Place Really Needs	26
Chapter 9	Twister	29
Chapter 10	Just When You Think You've Heard It All	32
Chapter 11	A Painful Realization	35
Chapter 12	Bath Time	37
Chapter 13	But They Have Great Wings	39
Chapter 14	Overflowing	42
Chapter 15	Toilet Paper and Johns	45

Chapter 16	Big Screen Debut	49
Chapter 17	Eternal Flame	54
Chapter 18	Taking Out the Trash	58
Chapter 19	Prayer Ninjas	62
Chapter 20	An Uplifting Experience	65
Chapter 21	Dive! Dive! Dive!	70
Chapter 22	Las Luces Azules	73
Chapter 23	Joking Around	77
Chapter 24	Searching for Leaders	81
Chapter 25	Beep, Beep!	85
Chapter 26	Legacy	88
Chapter 27	Generations	91
Chapter 28	Not the Last Word	94

Acknowledgments

This book would not be possible without the hundreds of young people who have invited me to be a part of their lives over the years. The blessings I've received from hanging out with all of you far outweigh anything I may have given in return.

Thank you to all my ministry partners over the past thirty-plus years. A few of you are named in this book; most of you aren't. Please don't read anything into that. It has been a tremendous privilege serving alongside all of you, and I thank you for the impact you've had on the kids we've served together. And on me.

To my parents, Stan and Ruth: thank you for being such incredible examples of character, integrity, and hard work, and for instilling in me the love of reading, writing, and storytelling.

My family has shared me with other people's kids for a very long time. Thank you to Luanne, Andrew, and Sam for your understanding, generosity, support, and occasional forgiveness. You are the best of the best.

Finally, thank you to God for this exhilarating journey. It's nothing I asked for or imagined, but I wouldn't trade it for anything.

Introduction

Do you want undeniable proof that God has a sense of humor? Here it is: he has invited me to play a role in building his Kingdom here on earth.

That's right. Flawed, broken, messed-up me.

I'm not being falsely modest when I say that I'm grossly inadequate for the task to which I've been called. Trust me. It's been independently verified. Over and over again.

In fact, over my more than thirty years of youth ministry I've been accused of being irreverent, unholy, inappropriate, misguided, and even vulgar. I suspect that this book may reinforce some of those opinions. Since you've made it past the title and have actually opened it, I'm hoping I have a chance of convincing you otherwise. In fact, I like to think that these accusations are overstated but, believe me, I'm far from perfect. Real? Yes. Authentic? I sure try to be. But never purposefully improper or impious.

All this puts me in pretty good company. I'm not in any way comparing myself to Jesus but, if you recall, he had accusers too. They used words like drunkard. Glutton. Blasphemer. Why? Because he went places deemed improper. He hung out with people considered unworthy. He said things judged controversial. His authenticity angered and offended those wanting something else.

What's my point, you ask? Throwing picnics on a hillside, attending weddings in a village, eating meals with outcasts, and having conversations with society's castaways made Jesus approachable. It made his Good News accessible. How else can you explain people in the street boldly reaching for him? Or a bunch of crazy guys cutting a hole in a roof so they could get their buddy seen by him?

This is the approach Jesus modeled for us. So why have we turned following him into something completely different? Why have we squeezed the joy out of living for him?

It's not my intent to downplay the importance of preaching and teaching, but that isn't the ministry God has called me to. I have been called to prepare the soil for planting. And sometimes that means stepping in manure.

Please don't misunderstand me. The challenge we face when being honest with ourselves about who we are, and real with other people, is making sure that we don't justify any and all activities in the name of ministry. We're warned, after all, about the consequences of leading our brother or sister into sin. There are lines that can't be crossed. The difficulty is that the line moves and we disagree about where it lies. So we do our best and we pray for discernment and wisdom and, more than occasionally, forgiveness.

I've found that ministry happens best as a part of real life. Authentic people are approachable. We experience joy in life's spontaneous moments. I believe that the vast majority of people are drawn to the Gospel not by words on a page, but by other folks living their lives as a celebration of the gift they've been given. It is through this initial attraction, and then through the cultivation of personal relationships, that most people are introduced to him. Christian activist and author Shane Claiborne has said, "The more I have read the Bible and studied the life of Jesus, the more I have become convinced that Christianity spreads best not through force but through fascination." I wholeheartedly agree. I've been forced to listen to far too many sermons that were far from fascinating. But Christians who live an authentic and inviting life overflowing with joy? Give me some of that.

Donald Miller, in his book *Blue Like Jazz*, puts it this way: "Sometimes you have to watch somebody love something before you can love it yourself. It's as if they are showing you the way."

Introduction

People who see Christianity as nothing more than a long list of Thou Shalt Nots are often intrigued by Christians who live their lives authentically. They won't experience that through folks who never leave their Sunday school classrooms.

Personal experience has proven this to me. Over the last thirty years I've done more than my share of preparing and planning. I have files full of talks that I've spent hours researching and writing and binders brimming with retreat instructions and mission trip devotionals. I've taught hundreds of lessons, led dozens of retreats, and guided scores of Bible studies. Yet ministry happens in the cracks. It happens in those unplanned, spontaneous, real-life experiences that are often messy and, believe it or not, don't usually include hymns or responsive readings. God often uses these moments of unplanned authenticity and community in ways that make our stumbling, fumbling, and bumbling efforts to further his Kingdom, well, funny. Hilarious, even.

So why risk proving my accusers correct by putting these stories to paper? I believe there are several reasons and, to keep things as clear as possible, I'll number them one through six below:

One: There's only ever been one perfect person in history, and none of us are Him. If these stories prove anything, it's that things will rarely—if ever—go the way you plan. Go ahead. Take a big sigh of relief. Knowing that you're not omnipotent should take a load off your shoulders. Although this fact doesn't in any way relieve of us the responsibility to do everything we do to the best of our ability, it's reassuring to be reminded that things will go wrong—and that God will do marvelous things regardless. If nothing else, these stories will assure you that when things go wrong you're not alone.

Two: Authenticity is attractive. Not in the physical sense, but from the standpoint of attracting attention and curiosity. One of the two criticisms I hear most often about Christianity is that Christians are hypocrites who don't live the life we profess. Being who we are—warts and all—is almost always refreshing and fascinating to those who expect something else. These stories will reinforce the idea that admitting our brokenness will break down barriers and provide us the opportunity to point to the source of our hope and joy.

Three: Redemption doesn't just take place after we're done breathing. God's work of renewal and restoration takes place in the here and now. Using broken people to further his Kingdom here on earth is a wonderful representation of that. These stories will remind us that Jesus can redeem even the most misguided and clumsy efforts of people just like you and me for his glory.

Four: God loves to use broken people to build His Kingdom. Moses. Gideon. Samson. Rahab. David. Jonah. Peter. Paul. God has a habit of using imperfect people to point us to him. By doing so, he reminds us of our need to rely on him. It also makes us more relatable to those around us; it frees us from thinking we need special qualifications to serve Him; and it protects us from the danger of boasting about "our" accomplishments.

Five: If teaching in parables was good enough for Jesus, then it's good enough for us. Believe me, I'm no great teacher. In fact, after having completed numerous spiritual gift assessments, I can tell you that teaching is *not* one of my gifts. These stories have value in and of themselves. But I also believe they contain lessons that extend beyond each individual story. I've done my best to use them to point out what I consider greater truths. If I've sometimes extended the metaphor beyond what seems plausible, well, forgive me for that as well!

Six: There is tremendous joy in being right where God has called you to be. I don't downplay the pain and suffering that may come your way as a follower of Jesus. Christ himself tells us that a life spent following him will require us to pick up our own cross. However, my desire is that these stories remind us to slow down and pay attention to what's happening all around us. After all my years of ministry I could be excused for thinking that I've seen it all. Having interacted with tens of thousands of kids it's easy to imagine that I've seen every authentic, unplanned, and unanticipated situation that there is to see. But just about the time that I find myself operating on autopilot, walking around half-lidded and disillusioned, I'm blessed with one of those wonderful, joyous,

Introduction

unexpected, where-did-that-come-from moments that reminds me of why I got into youth ministry in the first place. We should commit to doing our best to never miss a single one of the crazy, surprising, amazing, and joy-filled ways that Jesus helps us fulfill our purpose.

❊   ❊   ❊

Have you ever seen the painting of the laughing Jesus? I love that picture. And before you get all offended with me in the very first chapter of this book (believe me, you'll have plenty of opportunities for that later), I recognize the cultural inaccuracy of Westernized representations of Jesus. What I mean is, I love the emotion represented. I can't help but believe there were times, traveling the countryside with twelve young men, when things happened that caused Jesus to roar with laughter. Maybe even, you know, *Blazing Saddles* campfire scene kinds of things. After all, where do you think James and John got their nickname Sons of Thunder?

Is it irreverent to imagine that? I don't think so. After all, we're taught that Jesus was both fully God and fully human. Who's to say he didn't enjoy tickling Peter's nose with a reed while Peter was trying to sleep? I can even picture him trying to suppress a bit of a smile as he walked on water to his terrified disciples in the middle of a storm. And calling a guy who's been dead for three days out of his tomb, knowing he'd walk out like some stumbling mummy from a third-rate horror movie smelling like, well, death? Forget about it! After all my years of youth ministry, I've seen enough examples of his authenticity, approachability, and spontaneity to be convinced that Jesus loves to treat us to a great story and a good laugh. Do you doubt it? Then read on.

Chapter 1

That's Not Ministry

When word first started getting out about our youth center project, I was stopped in the commons after worship by one of the long-time members of my church at the time.

She was curious about what we were up to and had some questions. "Will you be delivering a message as part of the evening's activities?"

"No," I replied.

"Will you be asking the kids to join together in prayer at the beginning of the night?"

"Nope," I responded.

"Then you know what you're doing is not ministry, right?"

You don't say? Well, shoot. I guess we missed that.

The idea for a large community youth center was conceived while I was part of a local church youth ministry. God had blessed our youth programs with incredible growth, to the point where this growth played a significant role in our church needing to build a larger facility. As we spent time in our community, supporting kids at basketball games and band concerts, our leadership team agonized over the sheer number of kids we still weren't reaching. We talked and dreamed and prayed and finally realized that expecting those kids to make a first contact by walking through a church door was unrealistic. When Jesus said go and make disciples, he really meant the *go* part.

We knew we had to create something that didn't look, sound, or feel like church, but where kids could be part of a positive community and where we could shower them with God's love. So, to simplify a long and challenging process, we created a youth center with the mission of providing kids a safe, fun, and positive community where they could be physically active, socially engaged, and spiritually encouraged. A big part of this effort was the idea that we would be non-intimidating and non-pressuring when it came to matters of faith. We would not require kids to listen to a message. We would not demand they join us in prayer. That all seems so . . . transactional.

We.

Just.

Love.

Kids have responded. As I write this chapter, and since opening our doors nearly eleven years ago, we've had 30,362 individual kids visit us during our open-to-the-public hours. That's kids, not visits. Our annual attendance is also right around 30,000 visits per year. Over ten years. That's 300,000 opportunities to invest in a young person who has decided to visit us.

I don't say any of this to brag. Our goal from the start of this adventure has been to point the glory to God, not ourselves. Trust me when I say that if the success of this ministry depended on me we'd be in a world of hurt. Instead, I share this information to point out that perhaps loving people is enough.

It's not that we hide who we are or what we're about. Ask any kid who visits here and they know. And we don't shy away from discussions about faith. In fact, we celebrate them. Do we get to share the Gospel with each and every kid who walks through our doors? No. Do we wish we could? Yes. Are we learning to be content with the fact that we've been called to a ministry of outreach rather than discipleship? We're still working on that. But perhaps a ministry where God's love is shared without the expectation of anything in return is just refreshing enough to reach a generation that is tired of being constantly sold to.

Ralph Waldo Emerson famously said, "Your actions speak so loudly, I can not hear what you are saying." Jesus said, "This is how everyone will recognize that you are my disciples—when they see the love you have for each other" (John 13:35). It can be an ugly world out there, so we're doing our best to share a way of life that leads to meaning, purpose, hope, and joy. To be a little refuge of light in the darkness. By simply sharing God's love.

This approach has borne fruit. We know, for example, that 70 percent of the kids who visit our youth center claim no church home, meaning we're impacting kids who are not being reached by traditional youth ministry. We hear comments from kids who tell us that, "we're the first Christians they've met who actually do what we say we believe." We celebrate the number of young people who join our volunteer staff because of, as they tell us, the impact this place has had on their lives and their desire to pass that along. We look forward to the greetings we receive from regular visitors as they walk through our doors and hellos we get in the grocery store or at the local mall from kids who recognize us. We're blessed by the invitation to share the sorrows and joys of kids who open up to us on a regular basis. And this response shouldn't be surprising, right? After all, Jesus called us to be his witnesses. Not his defenders. I'm not aware of anyone who has ever been argued or coerced into a meaningful exploration of what it means to follow him.

I've run into other folks over the years who have also accused us of not being a ministry. And I know I'll stand in judgement someday, being held accountable for how I shepherded this resource for the furtherance of God's Kingdom. As I've made abundantly clear, I'm far from perfect. But I can say with all confidence that I'm not worried about that particular accusation. Bring it on.

Chapter 2

ALL I SAID WAS #*&$

I was walking through our youth center one evening when a group of girls approached me.

"That boy over there is using bad language," one of them said, while the others nodded their heads in earnest agreement.

This is not an uncommon occurrence. The young people who visit our building have bought into the idea of protecting this sanctuary from much of the junk they deal with in their everyday lives. They appreciate the safe environment we strive to provide and play an active role keeping things positive, so I was not surprised they were letting me know about something that made them uncomfortable. It happens all the time.

Because those of us who oversee things here can't be a part of every conversation and interaction in our facility, we value their help and follow up on every incident they bring to our attention. If we didn't, they'd soon realize they're wasting their time and quit letting us know what's going on.

After having them point out which boy they were talking about, I approached him, using all the de-escalation and non-intimidation techniques we've learned over the years.

"Hey buddy," I said. "I hear you've been using some inappropriate language."

He looked up at me with a confused look on his face, obviously trying to figure out what he said that might have offended someone. It actually took him several seconds to get there.

"All I said was #*%$," he replied.

To say that I was stunned is an understatement. In fact, I wasn't 100% sure of what I'd just heard. For one thing, my hearing isn't what it used to be. Second, loud music and louder voices in our facility can make it difficult to hear. Finally, I simply couldn't believe that particular word came out of that innocent looking 5th grader's mouth.

"What was that?" I asked.

"All I said was #*%$," he repeated. Reading the look on my face, he added, "We use that word at home all the time."

Now, I didn't just fall off the turnip truck. I realize the word he used, which begins with F, ends in C and K, and is not firetruck, does not possess the power it did when I was younger. In fact, I hear it used by people in everyday conversation nearly every time I sit in a booth at the local McDonalds or walk through the mall. It has entered the common lexicon. I'm also not judging. It's just that I don't find its use very . . . creative. Especially when used repeatedly in every sentence that comes out of someone's mouth.

That doesn't change the fact that for me, growing up, it was one of the most powerful and taboo words one could use. We didn't hear it often, so it still affects me like someone throwing a firecracker at my feet. And being tossed about so matter-of-factly by a cute little eleven-year-old with big brown eyes and a mop of messy hair made it even more disconcerting.

"Well, we don't use that word here," I replied. "Could you do me a favor and not use it again?"

"Sure, no problem," he said. "Anything else?"

"Nope, that's it," I answered. "Thanks." And that was the end of it. I didn't have to talk to him again that evening about his language.

The incident really stopped me in my tracks. I'm not a prude. Frankly, my wife has to occasionally scold me about the things that come out of my mouth. But I do worry about families that use language like that as a part of normal conversation – especially with their children. I love the quote from Spencer Kimball, a well-known former leader of the Mormon Church, who said, "Profanity is the effort of a feeble brain to express itself forcibly." There are more creative and less offensive ways for us to communicate.

I understand it's just a word. On the other hand, I also believe that words have incredible power. Out of respect for that power, there are words that we don't tolerate at our youth center. It's simply a matter of respecting those who are offended by profanity.

As is often the case, the impact of that brief encounter made an impression beyond those few moments of interaction. Although he certainly has no idea, that little guy gave me more than a tale to tell when we sit around sharing war stories. He gave me a book title.

Chapter 3

A Minty Fresh Buzz

Our church held a summer Kids' Camp program for more than twenty years. We trained our high school and college students to act as counselors and took our younger children away for a week of traditional camp activities. This camp experience led to more young people accepting Christ than any other ministry I've ever been a part of. The Holy Spirit was always a powerful presence during our years at camp.

In addition to times of worship and discipleship, we engaged in a number of goofy camp activities. One morning we decided to get the day started by involving our campers in a unique relay competition prior to breakfast. We organized them into teams based on their cabins, lined them up, and armed their counselors with squirt guns filled with mouthwash. The counselors squirted mouthwash into their campers' mouths, one at a time, and the campers then ran a short distance to a picnic table where they spat their mouthwash into a cup and then ran back to their line. The cabin that filled their cup first would be declared the winner. We thought it was a great idea, not only from the standpoint of goofy fun but also because it promoted good oral hygiene—which anyone who has spent time at camp with a bunch of kids knows is a definite bonus.

A Minty Fresh Buzz

At the end of the competition, after declaring a winner, I grabbed one of the cups used for the contest and stood on a picnic table, asking the assembled group of 150 or so campers and counselors if they'd like to see me drink the contents. You can imagine the response. I slugged down the contents to a deafening roar and, not surprisingly, the sound of some isolated retching. It was the kind of brazen act from which legends are made, and I can tell you that the story still comes up in conversation with people who were in attendance, twenty years or so after the fact.

There are a couple of things you should know. First, even I'm not stupid enough to drink a cup full of freshly spat mouthwash and saliva. In the chaotic aftermath of the competition, I substituted a fresh cup of mouthwash for one of the cups filled by the campers. This is the first time I've ever confessed my deception and I'm sure there will be people who read this book who will be disappointed to discover that my performance wasn't nearly as gross and disgusting as they thought.

Second, I forgot that most mouthwash contains about 25% alcohol, making it, yes, 50 proof. And I slammed back about ten ounces of it, or the equivalent of more than six shots. A couple of Listerinis without the olives. It took me a few minutes to figure out why I was feeling wobbly, light-headed, and unfocused until I realized that my cool mint cocktail had elevated my blood alcohol content to a get-pulled-over-and-walk-a-straight-line level. My self-satisfaction at my clever ruse was replaced with the horror of realizing I was buzzed at Kids' Camp. Fortunately, our period of free time after breakfast allowed me the opportunity to have a few cups of coffee and take a brisk walk around camp before I had to fulfill any of my ministry responsibilities.

Chapter 4

The Gales of October

Each fall we would take our church's senior high youth group on a weekend retreat to kick off the ministry year. We chose a theme for each retreat, and for several years running I based them on the popular television show *Survivor*. I divided our young people into tribes, devised a number of team-building competitions, and tied it all together using the competitions as object lessons meant to reinforce the spiritual theme of the weekend.

One year our retreat was at a camp near the shores of Lake Michigan in early October. We arrived on Friday evening and held some preliminary activities, enjoying the beautiful fall weather in Michigan. By Saturday morning when we awoke, the weather had turned gray, windy, and cold, feeling much more like November than early fall.

Our morning competition focused on spiritual gifts. I firmly believe you cannot put together an effective ministry team without a clear understanding of how the body of Christ is designed to work. The Apostle Paul uses the analogy of a human body to help us understand this concept. In a nutshell, he makes it clear that we are each designed to function in a unique way to further God's Kingdom, much like the different parts of the human body are designed to accomplish different functions. None of us are the body in its entirety, but instead we must work together to accomplish our calling. An effective ministry team, then, must include people with a broad and varied collection of spiritual gifts. Leadership. Intercession. Mercy. Discernment. Evangelism. Exhortation. The list goes on.

Spiritual gifts are discussed in several places in Scripture, most notably in chapter 12 of 1 Corinthians, but also in Romans 12, Ephesians 4, and 1 Peter 4. Although they are counted and named differently depending upon which Biblical scholar you read, most agree that there are twenty-three distinct spiritual gifts listed in scripture and that all believers are given at least one and often several of these individual gifts by God to glorify Him and serve others. There are a number of great books on this topic, but I strongly recommend Bruce Bugbee's *What You Do Best in the Body of Christ*.

Understanding the concept of spiritual gifts has helped me tremendously, not only in my personal life, but also as I have put various ministry teams together over the years. In fact, the team of adult leaders who served in our high school ministry at this particular time—a group of spiritually mature Christians who loved kids and were passionate about sharing Christ's love with them–were a perfect example of how the body of Christ functions when all the parts work together. Each had been recruited in part for the gifts they possessed, making sure that our team had everything necessary to best serve the young people placed in our care.

Back to our retreat. We created a competition meant to teach our group about the concept of spiritual gifts by having them design, construct, and operate a raft using some basic construction materials that I provided each tribe. My plan was to allow them to work as a team, using their various gifts and talents to help them succeed in their task. The idea was that the tribes would design and construct a raft that would support their entire group, launch it on the lake, paddle it to a small island in the middle, and then return to their starting point. Tribes would be awarded points based on their order of finish. My expectation was that during our debriefing after the competition we'd be able to talk about how the gifts of various team members – leadership, administration, craftsmanship, and others – played a role in each team's success and then use that as a metaphor for how we are meant to function as the body of Christ.

Given the change in weather conditions, I grabbed a couple of our adult leaders before breakfast, and we walked the short distance to the lake to decide whether or not we should cancel this particular competition. Each of our adult leaders was assigned to a different tribe. You should know that the adults took the competition very seriously. In fact, although I can't prove it, I suspect there was a fair amount of wagering between them on the outcome of the weekend's competition. There were most definitely rampant attempts at cheating.

When we got to the shore, I became very hesitant to hold the morning's competition. The temperature was in the low 50s, the wind was whipping, and the water was choppy. But my fellow adults convinced me that things were perfectly safe and that the conditions would simply add to the experience. Reluctantly, I agreed to proceed.

After breakfast we brought the students to the lakeshore, gave them their instructions, and set them to their task of building their rafts from the 55-gallon drums, two-by-fours, rope, and duct tape they were provided. After twenty minutes of design and building time, during which the weather continued to deteriorate, I once again consulted the adults about whether or not we should continue. Although a few of us—especially my wife—were hesitant, they convinced me to put the rafts in the water.

It took only a few minutes to recognize the error of my ways. The wind, when not gusting, was blowing at a steady twenty-five miles per hour and the small lake looked like Lake Superior during a November gale. The rafts were coming apart in the water at an alarming rate. Not surprisingly, Gordon Lightfoot's song "Wreck of the Edmund Fitzgerald" started running through my mind. Those of us left on shore reassured each other that everything was going to be alright, but more than half of the students were off their disintegrating rafts, bobbing in the cold water in their life jackets. After about ten minutes of fruitless attempts to come anywhere near the island where they were to collect their tribal flag and return to shore, I noticed from the corner of my eye that my wife was approaching me from across the beach. In addition to being a Registered Nurse, Luanne is a very even-tempered and mild-mannered woman. She has vast experience with me being an idiot and, as a result, has developed a great deal of tolerance for it. This time, she grabbed a handful of my jacket in two fists, pulled my face to within an inch of hers, and growled through clenched teeth, "You get those kids out of the water and you get them out now!!"

Even though I'm not the sharpest tool in the shed, I realized that it was time to call things off. After wiping the angry flecks of spit off my face from Luanne's face-to-face reprimand I blew my whistle, did my best to shout above the gale that the kids needed to come to shore, and sent our motorboat out to fetch them.

Not surprisingly, the students believed this was simply a part of the challenge and most of them refused to come in, continuing on in their losing battle to keep their rafts together and paddling toward their goal. We eventually had to force the last handful of them into the motorboat, getting the whole dripping and shivering bunch of them back to the lodge to warm up while the flotsam of their rafts washed against the eastern shore of the lake half a mile from where we began the challenge.

I can happily report that we avoided, by the slimmest of margins, any cases of hypothermia. And my object lesson about spiritual gifts became much more personal, with me as the central figure. Despite the fact that God has blessed me with the gift of leadership and had put me in a position to exercise it, not only had I caved in to peer pressure, but I had ignored the advice of people who were put on our team for the very purpose of exercising their own unique gifts.

Nearly twenty years later those involved still speak about this experience with a mixed sense of pride, amazement, and humor. I just make sure they don't do so within earshot of their parents.

Chapter 5

Speechless

Every summer our church takes its senior high youth group on a mission trip. We have found these trips to be powerful ways for students to deepen their relationship with Christ, build community, and develop a heart for service. We have served in places like New Orleans, Oklahoma City, Toronto, Chicago, Brooklyn, rural Tennessee, Atlanta, and a host of other locations.

Before we commit to a trip, we do a significant amount of research about the location and its sponsoring organization. Not only do we look for meaningful experiences for our young people, but we also want to be comfortable with the hosting organization and what they believe. But sometimes the best laid plans . . .

One year, we took a large group of students on a week-long trip to rural West Virginia. We felt as though we had been extremely diligent in our pre-trip research. It wasn't long after our arrival, however, that things began to go awry. On our first day one of the hosting organization's interns, during a conversation with one of our most spiritually mature young people, told her that all true Christians experience visions and if she had not yet experienced a vision then she hadn't made a true commitment to Christ. As you can imagine, our young student was shattered. We had significant repair to do, not only with her, but with our entire group as the story spread.

On the second day of our trip, as we returned to the school where we were staying after our day of work, our young men tried to enter the gymnasium where the guys were housed, only to find the doors locked. Upon pounding on the doors, one of the hosting group's interns emerged from the gym and shared with our group that she had locked us out because she felt Satan's presence there and felt the need to pray to remove him before letting us in. Nothing wrong with that, but it freaked more than a few of our young guys out. I found the head of our hosting organization and had a long talk with her about my concerns over the behavior of her interns and was assured that she'd have a discussion with them about their interaction with our students.

On our third evening, after showers and supper, we were participating in a time of worship led by the hosting group's worship leader. After just a couple of songs he stopped, told our group that we obviously weren't interested in properly worshipping Jesus, and kicked us out of the room in which we were gathered. I neither saw nor felt anything wrong with the worship that was occurring. Soon, the parking lot was full of students and leaders with confused, scared, deer-in-the-headlights expressions. It was the last straw in a very frustrating and difficult-to-understand couple of days.

I gathered the worship leader and the head of the hosting group and told them we needed to talk. As the three of us headed towards a quiet place to converse, one of my adult leaders–a guy who had helped lead at least 15 of these trips over the years–came up to me and said, "We're packing up and heading home, aren't we?" I replied that I thought probably so. Thinking about the rigors of a 16-hour drive back to Michigan, he responded, "I thought so . . . and I didn't get a shower today."

Once we found our quiet place, I explained our frustrations and concerns and told the hosting organization that I simply couldn't get my mind wrapped around what they were doing. I accused them of being manipulative. After a brief and emotional discussion, I could tell that the hosting organization's coordinator was frustrated with what had happened to that point and was sympathetic with my concerns. "Are you going home?" she asked.

"I don't know," I said.

"What are you going to say to the kids?" she asked.

"I don't know," I responded. And I didn't. It was such a raw and confusing experience that, for one of the first times in my life, I had no idea what I was going to say.

I left the room where we were meeting and walked across the parking lot, praying for guidance, and was surprised to find that our group was no longer congregated in the lot. There were lights on in the room that we had been kicked out of half an hour earlier, so I walked in that direction. As I entered, I discovered our group in a large circle, holding hands and praying. And, most amazingly, at the very moment I entered the room, one of our young female students was praying for the leaders of the hosting organization.

I was floored. What extraordinary maturity from a 17-year-old girl, praying for the people who had so frustrated and confused us. I stood and joined them in prayer until they noticed my presence and wrapped up. I've never seen so many faces looking at me with the expectation that I was going to make everything all right. We sat down and I spoke to the group for about twenty minutes. To this day, I don't really know what I said, but at the end of my effort to comfort and reassure them, I invited the students and leaders to share their feelings and concerns. We spent more than an hour–and a lot of tears–talking through what we had experienced so far that week.

After everyone had been given the opportunity to share, I asked a couple of questions. My first was this: "If I had asked you an hour ago if you wanted to pack up and go home, how many of you would have wanted to do that?" Every single hand in the room was raised. My second question, which was infinitely more risky, was: "How many of you want to go home now?" If even one hand went up, I had a problem, but not a single hand was raised. God's power and presence in that room was palpable. We talked a bit more about how we were going to move forward and then called it a night. Because of how we were forced to circle our wagons and come together as a group, the rest of our week was an amazing experience. The emotional rawness broke down barriers between us. Our students gained confidence in their own spiritual maturity. Our adults rose to leadership levels they may not have known they possessed. We were challenged to examine our individual beliefs. And we all learned how to respond in love to those who hurt us.

Is this how I envisioned the week was going to go? Was that the way the trip would have gone had it been up to me? Would I want to go through that kind of experience again? The answer to each of these questions is no. However, to this day when we talk about that trip, we are reminded about how God can use difficult and painful experiences for His Glory. And, every bit as important, for our growth.

Chapter 6

Who Did You Say Is in Charge?

I was sitting in a room full of a dozen or so ministry partners one day, discussing the trials and challenges of youth ministry. In my position as a church youth director, I was responsible for all children from 3 years old through high school. That day we were talking about junior high ministry. I casually mentioned that although I valued all my ministry volunteers, I had a special place in my heart for those who chose to hang out with junior highers. To survive, let alone thrive, in an environment with more hormones than brain cells takes a special kind of person. Plus, the smell. Imagine a fifty-fifty mix of vinegar and Axe body spray assaulting your nostrils. I had always been a senior high guy and couldn't imagine spending time in that environment. As a compliment to my junior high leaders I told the group that "You'll never catch me dead in a room full of junior highers."

Talk about an utter lack of humility. And believe me, I know better. There have been numerous times in my life when God has had to remind me that I'm not the one setting the agenda. Still, and more than occasionally, stupid stuff comes out of my mouth for which I pay later.

Who Did You Say Is in Charge?

The Bible is full of warnings about pridefulness. Proverbs 11:12 says, "when pride comes, then comes disgrace, but with the humble is wisdom." 1 Peter 5:5 tells us, "God opposes the proud but gives grace to the humble." Most importantly, the entire life of Jesus is a lesson in humility. Yet there I was, declaring for everyone to hear that I was the one charting my own path. Looking back, I can picture God in heaven, surrounded by his angels, his ears perking up when I made that statement. I can imagine him smiling, looking around at the assembled host, asking, "Did you hear what he just said? Does he really think he's in charge??" I can then picture him rubbing his hands together and chuckling, inviting those in his presence to "watch this."

Fast forward a few years to my new position as director of a community youth center. In addition to the activities and events we hold, we are open to 7th and 8th grade students on Friday evenings. Yes, I now spend my Friday evenings surrounded by several hundred of my closest junior high friends. I imagine God looking down upon me during these crazy and chaotic Friday evenings, daring me to make some other bold and foolish declaration.

I am currently working very hard to eliminate the word 'never' from my vocabulary. In fact, I hope to never use it again.

Chapter 7

RISING ABOVE THE DARKNESS

We experienced the first power outage at our youth center during our open-to-the-public hours on a Wednesday evening. We were about an hour into the evening when the lights went out due to a storm in the area. Our emergency lighting came on immediately and, after a few shouts of surprise, things calmed down and our staff was able to have a brief discussion with each other about how to proceed. Since the kids didn't seem concerned, we believed we could keep them safe and, because it's a significant undertaking to arrange to send everyone home, decided to remain open and make the best of the situation.

Of course, we made some adjustments. We now had several hundred junior high students in a large building mostly lacking light. Recognizing that the darkness can sometimes foster inappropriate behavior, we closed off portions of the building in an effort to bring everyone together and keep everyone in sight. Knowing that we needed to be extra alert and aware, we reassigned staff, moving many from support roles to supervisory positions. Matt, our enterprising Person in Charge that evening, made a quick trip to the local store, picked up a couple hundred glowsticks, brought them back to our facility, and distributed them to everyone. By recognizing the threat, remaining vigilant, coming together as a group, and spreading our little individual lights throughout the building, we overcame the darkness and created a memorable evening.

It's not hard to tell where this one is going, right?

Jesus spent a fair amount of time talking about light and darkness. Not only did he refer to himself as the light of the world, he exhorted us to be the same. A lamp on a stand. A city on a hill. We have been called to illuminate a better way. In a world filled with strife it's our responsibility to reveal a path that leads to hope, meaning, peace, belonging, and joy. And how does Jesus instruct us to do this? By letting others see our good deeds so that God can be recognized as the one who offers this alternative.

As a ministry that aspires to be a light in our community, this message resonates and inspires. One of the goals we speak of regularly is this: as kids are leaving our facility we want them to be thinking, "That place felt different. I'd like to find out why." If, through the way we love those who visit us we have pointed them to God, then we've fulfilled our call to be light.

As students were leaving at the end of the night a number of them asked if we could turn off the lights again next week. Our response was, "Ummmm, no!" We had no interest in inviting the darkness to become a regular visitor. It was comforting, though, to know that we had the tools we needed to defeat it when it presented itself.

Chapter 8

WHAT THIS PLACE REALLY NEEDS

During a Saturday evening not long ago one of our 5th grade visitors stopped me next to one of our youth center's basketball courts. Looking up, and without preamble, she asked me, "Do you know what this place really needs?"

That question always stops me in my tracks.

To remain as fresh and relevant as possible we continually seek visitor feedback and are always ready to listen when one of our guests is willing to give us their opinion. Plus, encouraging kids to be an active part of our community is vital. It promotes a sense of belonging, which is a critical aspect of our effort to create a safe, fun, and encouraging community for the kids who visit us.

American psychologist Abraham Maslow argued that we are motivated by the fulfillment of our most basic needs. In addition to fundamental needs like food, water, warmth, and rest, Maslow defined other needs, including our desire for a sense of belonging. The need to belong shouldn't surprise us. It's why we love to wear our favorite team gear. It's a big part of why gangs flourish. And it's why we seek places, to borrow from an iconic 1980s television show, where everybody knows our name.

What This Place Really Needs

The COVID-19 crisis has had a tremendous impact on kids, in part because it stripped away many of the places they went to experience belonging. In addition to what we are seeing with our own eyes during this time of increased social isolation, the U.S. Centers for Disease Control and Prevention have reported that emergency department visits for children's mental health-related reasons have increased dramatically during the time of the pandemic.

A study published in 2010 by the National Recreation and Park Association entitled *The Rationale for Recreation Services for Youth* clearly outlined the importance of what they termed out-of-school-time youth programs. They found that such programs:

- reduce juvenile delinquency
- increase positive and reduce negative behaviors
- expose youth to less violence
- improve children's educational performance
- help to decrease health care costs
- increase the economic contributions of young people when they become adults
- help youth develop self-confidence, optimism, and initiative

Lacking a positive alternative, we'll settle for almost any way to find our place. As kids increasingly suffer the isolating effects of screen time, the need for a place where they can be physically active, socially engaged, and spiritually encouraged is more critical than ever. We are created to be in community. Heck, even God exists in community with Jesus and the Holy Spirit!

Back to our young visitor who wanted to share her opinion with me on what our youth center really needed.

"Why don't you tell me what you think we need." I smiled with encouragement.

"Penguins," she replied, like it was the most obvious answer in the world. Unblinking. Deadly serious.

All I Said Was #*%$

My mind immediately went to the consequences of having a roving colony of penguins in our building. Penguins being tossed back and forth over the volleyball net. Penguins on skateboards. Penguins demanding anchovies on their pizza. Penguin diapers.

She must have realized that she had lost me for a moment because she immediately added, "Wouldn't that be the coolest thing ever?"

I couldn't argue with that. "Yeah, it would!" I replied. But having had a minute to think, I was pretty sure I had found an out. "But where would we get them?"

"The internet," she replied without missing a beat. "You can buy anything there." And away she ran, on to her next adventure.

Just to be sure, I typed *penguins* into the search box on the Amazon website the following Monday morning. I found stuffed penguins, penguin books, penguin duct tape, and even penguin Pez dispensers, but no live penguins.

I'm hoping they become available around the same time that Amazon starts using flying drones to make their deliveries. How cool would it be to see a penguin flying above our city on the way to its new home at our youth center? And forget about us. What about that penguin? After millions of years of flightless existence, that little guy would be the Orville Wright of his species.

No penguins yet. But you never know.

Chapter 9

TWISTER

We were within an hour of home in the late afternoon, returning from one of our week-long summer mission trips; there were 40 or so students on our church bus and a couple of vans full of students following. As we drove through Kalamazoo, Michigan, the skies turned as dark as I've ever seen them during the daytime and the rain came down in sheets so dense that we couldn't see more than twenty or thirty feet past the hood of our bus. While my friend Tim drove, I stood at the front of the bus and tried to tune the radio to a local station to find out what was going on. At that moment my wife, who knew approximately where we were, called to warn me that there was a tornado on the ground near Kalamazoo. Students' cell phones (this was before smartphones) began to ring as well. It didn't take everyone long to figure out that we were directly in the tornado's path.

Since we were on the interstate, we didn't have the option of finding a building in which to seek shelter. Students were praying and singing softly to themselves as we crept along the highway, straining to see through the darkness and rain. Tim and I nervously discussed what to do, finally deciding that we were going to have to pull to the shoulder and put everyone under the bus.

Just then we caught a glimpse of lighter sky to the north. Tim said, "Forget it, we're gonna drive out of this thing!" Giving the bus as much gas as he dared, he plowed ahead toward lighter skies and ultimately outraced the storm.

As the rain subsided and relief washed over us all, Tim started to laugh. Hard. Looking at me, he said, "Stan, do you know the craziest thing about what just happened?"

With a number of possibilities running through my brain, I answered, "No, Tim, why don't you tell me?"

"Do you realize that with the worst weather and visibility imaginable, we just had the one-eyed guy driving the bus through it?"

Did I forget to mention that Tim lost an eye as a young man in a freak automotive repair accident?

I'm not sure if it was relief over being through the storm or the irony of the moment, but I can't remember the last time I've laughed that hard. Our students might have been a bit concerned for our sanity. The truth is that Tim had spent a number of years as a professional truck driver and he was absolutely the best guy to have in the driver's seat at that particular moment. But the irony was still hilarious.

Talk about seeing through a glass darkly.

Back when we first felt called to create a large community youth center in our hometown, we had hoped to find a contractor who was sympathetic to our cause and who might, among other things, allow us to utilize volunteer labor to remodel the 34,000-square-foot building we had acquired. Unfortunately, we couldn't find anyone to accommodate that construction model so we tackled the project ourselves. We worked through the rezoning process, pulled our own permits, put together a crew of hired help and volunteers, and spent six months turning a former plastic injection molding factory into a place for kids.

Throughout that summer of remodeling my friend Joel (a long-time ministry partner and fellow co-founder of the youth center project) and I would occasionally look at each other in the midst of our $1.4 million dollar remodel and ask, "What happens if we do all this and only thirty kids show up?"

Oh, we of little faith.

Twister

We finished construction and held our soft opening in late November 2010. Within ten weeks of opening and with almost no promotion (we were hoping for a very slow growth curve) we had a Friday night with five hundred junior high students in attendance. Within a couple of months we had consecutive Friday evenings with eight hundred and fifty junior-highers in our building.

To quote a popular 1980s movie: if you build it, they will come.

What do these stories have in common?? Whether you're driving a bus trying to figure out where the weather clears or undertaking an entirely new adventure to share God's love with young people in your community, God rarely reveals His entire plan. Instead, as Psalm 119:105 says, God's word is a "lamp unto my feet, and a light unto my path." Not a spotlight into the distance. As much as we wish he'd show us the future, that wouldn't require much faith, would it? So we take things one step at a time, trusting in his promises to take care of us and to do immeasurably more than we can imagine.

In conclusion, let me share this truth: having lived through both experiences described in this chapter I can report with full conviction that surviving a building filled with several hundred junior high students can be very much like, well . . . driving a church bus through a tornado.

Chapter 10

Just When You Think You've Heard It All

I was hosting an organization that had rented our youth facility one evening when an adult approached me and said, with no introduction, "Excuse me. There's a turd on the basketball court."

Despite what my wife claims, I'm occasionally capable of entertaining more than one line of thought at a time. This was one of those times.

First, I need to be honest. Turd. I hadn't heard that word in a long time. I hear many other words used to describe the end result of the act of defecation, but turd? I laughed reflexively. That word just appeals to that junior high guy part of my brain that (sorry) all men still possess. In fact, I'm snickering even as I write this.

Second (thought number two, if you will), I experienced the "Wait, what?" response. Our basketball court had been in use all evening long and, in fact, the guy talking to me had just left the current game because of the poop in the paint. How could it be possible that there was a turd on the court? He must have been mistaken. Maybe it was a partially chewed bit of tootsie roll that had fallen out of someone's mouth or something like that.

"A what?" I asked.

"A turd," he said. "Someone crapped on the court."

Just When You Think You've Heard It All

I couldn't imagine that it was possible but, not wanting to pooh-pooh his concern, I jumped off my stool, followed him onto the court and, lo and behold, discovered caca on the court. A deuce of the non-shooting variety. Something truly foul. I was flabbergasted. I looked around and asked the guys on the court what had happened but, in a lifetime filled with asking silly questions, that was easily one of the dumbest I've ever asked. Who was going to own up to that?

You probably already know that if you're going to lead a ministry you're going to have to deal with some crap—although more likely figurative than literal. It's unavoidable. We live in a "gotcha" culture in which people actively search for ways to point out the shortcomings of others in a misguided effort to feel better about themselves. If I had a dollar for every unsigned note of criticism that's been slipped under my office door over the years I'd have quite a lot of dollars.

This culture, combined with what's been called an addiction to offense, has led to toxic behavior. Because of my need to simplify things, I've boiled it down to my belief that there are two kinds of people in the world: those who reach up to tear others down and those who reach down to pull others up. I know which people I admire. Which I prefer to associate with. Which I aspire to be. And this I know for certain:

I am broken and will make mistakes.

Other broken people will seek to point out my brokenness in ways meant to hurt me.

I can't change this.

So what do we do? I have a quote by 19th century artist and philosopher Elbert Hubbard hanging over my desk that says, "To avoid criticism do nothing. Say nothing. Be nothing." Those of us called to ministry know that doing nothing is not an option. God has called us to *do* things. We will be criticized. To put it in Old Testament terms, you'd best gird your loins and prepare for the haters. That's the first thing to do: understand what's going on and realize it's a price of responding to God's call. One of the crosses we'll be expected to bear.

Second, we need to discern who to listen to. Those unsigned notes slipped under my door? I decided early on that if the note wasn't signed, I wouldn't read it. And social media? It's a viral version of the unsigned note. Social media is mostly a cesspool of passive aggressive rubbish posted by people who lack the courage to address you face to face. There are people in our lives who love us, who want the best for us, and who, through relationship, have earned the right to guide and correct us. Listen to them. Ignore the rest.

Finally, you need to remember what got you to the point of being criticized in the first place. You have responded to an invitation by God himself to join him in building his Kingdom here on earth. The creator and sustainer of the universe, who loves you passionately and who holds you in the palm of his hand, has called you to his work. There is purpose and meaning and contentment and joy that comes with responding to that call. Consign the rest to, well, wherever crap belongs.

Back to the turd on the court. Presented with no alternative, I spent a moment trying to picture the physics of how it could have gotten to where it was, intact, but to this day I'm unable to imagine the process from point of origin to final resting place. Thankfully, I guess. Apparently, despite numerous obstacles, gravity ultimately wins. Regardless, I gloved up, masked up, manned up, grabbed some cleaning supplies, and removed the offending excrement from the court so that the game could resume.

Something new to add to my job description. I'm just not sure how to word it.

Chapter 11

A Painful Realization

For the first few years that our youth center was open we offered an activity called *reball*. It was a form of indoor paintball that we played in a 5,000-square-foot portion of our building. It used all the same equipment as paintball except that the projectile was a reusable rubber ball rather than a ball filled with paint. Reusable ball. Reball.

Since reballs travel at 180 feet per second, they can leave a pretty impressive welt. I was standing outside our building one evening after our open-to-the-public hours for high school students, waiting for kids to get picked up, when I noticed a young lady with a particularly ugly reball welt on her neck.

Engaging her in conversation, I said, "Wow, that musta hurt."

"Worst thing ever," she replied.

"Maybe not," I answered. "Worst thing ever might be trying to explain that mark to your parents."

Now, I realize that some of the things I say have a way of going over the heads of the kids I'm talking to. And I could see by the way her eyes were moving back and forth in her head that she was trying to figure out what I meant. But then her eyes stopped, locked onto mine, and got reaaallllly wide as she grasped my meaning. For those of you not tracking, she had realized that the mark looked like a Guinness Book of World Records hickey.

"Ummm," she said. "If I need my dad to call you and, like, verify how I got this, would it be okay?"

"Of course." I gave her one of my business cards so she'd have my number. Obviously, she was thinking she might need someone to confirm her story that she got the mark from playing reball and not from, you know, the other way.

I never heard from her dad. Too bad. I would have enjoyed helping him figure things out. After all, a sincere search for the facts seems to be a rare thing these days. Frankly, I can't remember a time in my life when distortion—and outright lying—has been not only acceptable but has devolved into an art form. A reliance on false prophets whose only expertise is their ability to gain followers of their social media accounts has replaced the honest effort to determine and rely upon the things in our life that are observable and repeatable. Propaganda— telling a lie, making it big, and repeating it often—rules.

Sadly, church folk seem to be among the loudest voices in this cacophony of foolishness. I am embarrassed for my brothers and sisters who have joined in this rejection of the facts. For a group of people who profess to follow the one who proclaimed himself the Truth, this is baffling and shameful. If we aspire to be more like him, we must reject that which is false, misleading, or fake. Yet here we are.

If all this feels as though it's hitting close to home, so be it. Sometimes the truth hurts.

Very much like a reball to the neck.

Chapter 12

Bath Time

One summer we took a group of 50 or so senior high students on a mission trip to Acuña, Mexico. After enjoying an air-conditioned airplane ride from Grand Rapids, Michigan to San Antonio, Texas and collecting our luggage in the cool comfort of the San Antonio airport, we exited the terminal to find our rental vans and head to the border. The 110-degree Texas heat assaulted us in a way that was shocking to a bunch of Midwesterners who rarely experienced anything over 90 degrees. The heat had a weight to it that pushed down on us as we walked across the black asphalt. There seemed to be no oxygen available to breathe as we dragged our luggage across the soft blacktop. But we made it to our vans, piled in, fired up the air-conditioning—which took away only the most brutal edge of the heat—and headed a couple of hours south.

Conditions did not change during our time south of the border. We were tasked with mixing mortar and laying the block walls for a church under construction. It was hot, sweaty, and dusty work and the kids accomplished a lot in very trying circumstances.

There was no running water on our jobsite, however, and, after a couple of days of working in temperatures in excess of 115 degrees, things were getting pretty funky. We asked our hosts if there was somewhere we could get a shower.

"Not really," they responded. "We could load up the vans and go down to the river for a swim, though."

At that point, any opportunity to cool off and clean up sounded wonderful, so we readily agreed. After dinner we put on our swimsuits, loaded into our vehicles, and took off for the river.

As many of our group's activities seemed to do, our drive degenerated into a competition between our youth leaders over who could arrive there first. As our vans travelled single-file down a dusty two-track toward our destination, one of our drivers decided he saw a shortcut. Despite signs with words like "Aviso!" and "Peligro!" and, if memory serves, "Propiedad de Militares Mexicanos," he took off cross-country. Only later did we find out that his path took him across a Mexican military firing range. Gives a whole new meaning to the phrase "driving while bombed."

Anyway, our vehicles all arrived safely at the river, which ended up being the Rio Grande, by the way. We tumbled out of the vans and sprinted to the water, carrying our bottles of shampoo and bars of soap. This, fortunately, was before the days when running into this particular river might provoke an international incident.

Best.

Bath.

Ever.

Despite the fact that there was a small herd of cows wading in the water a couple hundred yards upstream and that we couldn't see our hands six inches below the surface of the muddy water (I use the adjective 'muddy' optimistically, given the proximity of the cows), everyone had the opportunity to get clean and refreshed. In fact, we made the trip to the river a couple additional times during our time in Mexico for the sake of group hygiene. So a bunch of folks from a city on the banks of the Grand River in Michigan enjoyed several opportunities for refreshment in another river named Grand nearly 1,500 miles from home. Seems fitting, right?

Chapter 13

BUT THEY HAVE GREAT WINGS

Let me tell you why I don't believe in conspiracies: there is no such thing as a secret. Ben Franklin put it this way: "Three may keep a secret, if two of them are dead."

In this day and age of television shows like *60 Minutes,* journalists looking to earn a Pulitzer Prize by exposing the most recent scandal, and a society bent on exposing the weaknesses and foibles of others, we are living in an anti-secret society. I think it takes way more faith to believe that people could keep the kind of secret that involves faking the moon landing than it does to believe we have the technology to put a man on the moon.

I could give you many examples that demonstrate how I've arrived at this conclusion. Here's one. Sharing it is going to sting a little.

Another mission trip. This time Atlanta. Later in our week of serving, we decided to give the kids a night off from ministry work. We took them to a local shopping and entertainment area, gave them each enough cash to purchase a meal, and told them they were on their own for a couple of hours (with each group having an adult leader join them, of course). We told them to find a restaurant of their own choosing and enjoy something other than the hot dogs and macaroni and cheese that are standard fare on such trips.

As I wandered the shopping area alone, I noticed one of our groups—our senior boys and a couple of adult leaders—standing outside a restaurant, preparing to enter. This particular establishment is known for its owl logo and scantily-clad waitresses. I hustled toward the group, surprised by the fact they thought this was an appropriate place for them to eat their evening meal.

"What're you thinking, guys?" I asked, as I approached them.

Looking a bit downcast at my materialization, one of the guys said, "It's no big deal, Stan. They have great wings!"

At that point, I could have taken advantage of several teaching opportunities. I could have talked about our responsibility to reflect righteousness. I could have discussed the objectification of women. But instead, my response was, "OK, but you're not going in there without me."

Idiot.

What made me think that joining them resolved the situation? I'd like to say that weariness played a role. At this point in the week, operating on about four hours of sleep a night, I'd like to think I could be excused for exercising terrible judgement. But I am reminded of something else Ben Franklin said: "He that is good for making excuses is seldom good for anything else."

Please understand that I'm not judging. If you frequent this establishment, it's none of my business. Knock yourself out. But in this instance, with this group of young men, and in my position of responsibility, this was absolutely the wrong decision.

After our meal, before we gathered ourselves to leave, I looked at each of the boys and swore them to secrecy about our visit. Another red flag that this was a terrible choice, right? I said something like, "Guys, I'm being completely serious when I say no one can know that we ate here. People won't understand, and we'll all be in trouble when we get home—not only from your parents, but likely our church leadership as well. You each need to look me in the eyes and promise me that you won't say anything about this." Each guy earnestly promised they'd never say a word.

Later that evening all our groups met back at the church bus to return to our lodging for the week. The half-dozen senior boys who I had dined with got on the bus first, of course, since they had staked out the back seats of the bus. I stood near the door as the kids all filed on, waiting until everyone was on board to take my place in the driver's seat. What happened next is exactly as it happened, without exaggeration. I stood at the front of the bus, counted heads, sat in my seat, buckled my seat belt, and before I could turn the key in the ignition the freshman girl sitting in the seat behind me leaned forward and said, "Stan, did you hear the senior boys ate at Hooters?"

Less than two minutes. Thirteen rows of seats. Sworn to absolute secrecy.

There is no such thing as a secret.

There were, of course, ramifications when we returned home from the trip. Nothing formal, but certainly a few informal conversations about my lapse in judgement. And, certainly, more ammunition for those who deemed me unworthy of my position in the first place. It definitely served as a reminder to me of the importance of continually pursuing a higher standard.

Deep state? Flat earth? Area 51? Bigfoot? A restaurant where little is concealed has made it difficult for me to believe in anything that depends upon a large group of people keeping something, you know . . . covered up.

Chapter 14

Overflowing

As you might imagine, a 34,000 square foot youth center filled with hundreds of kids can be a noisy, smelly, chaotic place where there is never a shortage of tasks needing attention. As I walked through the facility on a busy Friday evening I noticed an especially long line at our café and our staff struggling to keep up so I thoroughly washed my hands (I originally wrote 'quickly' rather than 'thoroughly' but realized our food inspector might read this) and asked if I could help out by pouring some sodas.

I'll confess that I love doing this job. It's a break from my normal responsibilities which are often equal parts referee, fireman, and sheriff. I'm able to focus on the mundane task of filling cups with ice and pop (yes, I'm from Michigan), zoning out for a few minutes amid the pandemonium of kids who run everywhere they go, scream everything they say, and touch everybody and everything with which they come into contact.

Until a melodic refrain broke through my reverie.

"What would you like, tonight, sweetie?"

"That'll be two dollars, hon."

"Don't forget your change, darlin.'"

Over and over again, my friend and co-worker Ronda interacted with the kids who stepped up to her register, showering them with terms of affection. Hon. Sweetie. The occasional *darlin'*.

Overflowing

A few *buddies*. Pouring over the kids like the pop in the cups I was filling that occasionally spilled onto my hands, the residue of her words clinging to them just like sticky soda did to me.

I stood and listened for a while, not wanting to break the spell. I've known Ronda for a long time and I know what she was doing was neither from a desire to perform nor a sense of obligation. It was simply God's love bubbling out of her onto the kids. It was, as Jesus said in John 10:10, abundant life overflowing. A sweet song.

When we finally got to the end of the line of kids waiting to be served, I stepped over to Ronda and asked if she realized the power of her words. "These kids," I told her, "get called a lot of things in the course of their everyday lives and, for many of them, it's often the opposite of hon, sweetie, or darlin'. I can't tell you how blessed I feel to have heard a little bit of it."

Ronda, of course, deflected the praise and thanked me for my words. As I walked away I couldn't help thinking about the impact of simple things. We sometimes get hung up on the idea that only big ministry matters and, if we can't go big, we might as well not try at all. But big ministry is often lots of small acts of service piled together. In fact, big and small are terrible words to connect to ministry. Here's the truly beautiful thing: we don't have to worry about things like big, small, the attendance numbers at our youth group meetings, or whether or not anything we've said to that particularly troubled kid we see every week has sunk in. Our responsibility is simply to be obedient to God's call and to work at it with all our heart. The apostle Paul, in his first letter to the Corinthians, put it this way:

> *I planted the seed and Apollos watered it, but God made it grow. So neither he who plants nor he who waters is anything, but only God, who makes things grow.*

That doesn't mean we don't have a responsibility. Scripture also instructs us that "whatever you do, work at it with your whole being, for the Lord and not for men" (Colossians 3:23). We can't simply sit around thinking that building God's Kingdom here on earth doesn't require our all. But the bottom line is this: if we're faithful and obedient, we can trust that the results are in God's hands. So at the end of a long day, as you're driving home agonizing over whether or not anybody paid any attention to the lesson you spent all week preparing, you can take comfort in the truth of the idea that we do our best and God does the rest. That takes a bit of the pressure off, right?

We've all experienced the power of a smile, a thank-you, a pat on the shoulder, or being called by name. At the end of the day, the impact of a huge community youth center is not the result of the size of the building or the number of kids who attend. Rather, it's the accumulation of all the simple acts of compassion and service that occur within. It's exactly as Jesus says in John 13:35: "This is how everyone will recognize that you are my disciples—when they see the love you have for each other."

As I was reminded by God's love flowing through Ronda in our café.

Chapter 15

TOILET PAPER AND JOHNS

I was startled awake by my wife Luanne calling my name.
"Stan!" heard her say as I struggled to understand what was going on. "Stan, there's someone at our door!"

At that point the ringing doorbell registered with me—the single chime that indicated that someone was in our garage.

"Someone's in the garage!" I said to her. Well done, Captain Obvious.

"Go see what's going on." There was a note of alarm in her voice.

"By myself?" I responded, displaying the courage and fortitude any man wants to demonstrate to his bride.

"We'll go together," she answered.

Noting that our clock glowed one am, we climbed out of bed and made our way downstairs through our dark house, the doorbell continuing to ring incessantly. As we arrived at the door from our garage into our house, we stopped. "Who's there?" I yelled.

"Stan, it's Jon and John," a frantic voice replied. "Let us in!"

Recognizing the voice as belonging to one of the boys in our high school youth group, I opened the door to indeed find Jon and John in our garage. The panicked looks on their faces registered only briefly as my attention was drawn behind them to an almost impenetrable curtain of toilet paper blanketing everything in my garage. Both cars were wrapped in toilet paper like huge Christmas gifts. Toilet paper was wrapped in and through wire shelving. Toilet paper dangled from every possible hanging spot and covered every object. A masterpiece. A toilet paper Picasso. A Charmin Chagall. A White Cloud Warhol. OK, I'll stop, but that art history class I had to take as a part of my liberal arts education was really starting to pay off there.

My attention was drawn back to the boys standing at my door, wondering why, after such a successful prank, they'd turn themselves in.

"You gotta let us in," they pleaded. "The cops are outside and we can't leave!"

Luanne, being the merciful one in our relationship, invited them in. She offered them a cookie and something to drink in an effort to calm them down while I walked through our still-dark house to our living room window. Sure enough, there were two officers on the sidewalk across the street in the company of one of our neighbors, shining their flashlights into backyards in an obvious search for something.

"Yup," I said, enjoying the moment maybe a bit too much. "The cops are definitely out there."

"What do we do?" asked Jon, or maybe it was John, their panic once again rising to the surface.

"We'll just hang out until they leave, and then you guys can take off," answered Luanne.

"We probably ought to clean things up," they said sheepishly.

"Good idea," I answered. We walked back toward the garage. As we stepped through the doorway one of the boys, without thinking, flipped on the light switch.

Oops.

Light spilled through the glass panes of our garage door as the boys began their cleanup and, in less than sixty seconds, we heard a tapping at the side service door. I opened the door to see two police officers, one slightly behind the other, both with their hands on the holsters.

"Are you the homeowner?" one of them asked.

"Yes I am." I answered, noticing that all efforts at cleaning had stopped as the boys froze in place.

"Everything OK here?" the office asked.

"It is," I replied. "Just a little prank."

"Mind if we step inside?" asked the second officer.

"Not at all. Come on in," I said, again enjoying how this situation was unfolding.

The cops took in the boys' handiwork, slight smiles forming at the corners of their mouths. Did I mention it was a Scott Seurat? A two-ply Toulouse-Lautrec?

Looking at the boys, the first officer asked, "So which of you lives in Marne?"

New panic. The cops had located the boys' car parked in the street a few houses to the east and had run the plates.

"I do," stammered Jon, as both boys were now probably envisioning scenes from *The Shawshank Redemption*.

"Well, just so you know," continued the officer, "since this was called in we'll have to file a report. It won't go any further than that but we'll have your names should we run into either of you again."

"Yes sir," both boys eagerly responded, relief washing over their faces.

The officers left, the clean-up was finished, and the boys prepared to leave. "Sorry about all this," offered John.

"It's okay guys," Luanne said from the doorway into our house. "Just promise me you'll drive safe on your way home." My ever-merciful wife.

As I walked them out of the garage, the less compassionate half of the married couple said, in a voice not meant for Luanne to hear, "Just remember. I own you now." And I sent them on their way.

The next morning I walked outside to grab the morning paper. My neighbor, whose name is – wait for it – John, caught my attention from across the street.

"What was going on last night?" he asked.

"Oh, just kids being kids," I responded. "No big deal."

"I saw the car go up and down the street a few times with its lights off and thought I should call the cops," John responded. "My wife said not to, that it was probably just some of your youth group kids, but I thought better safe than sorry."

"John," I replied, smiling, "you just keep on calling them every time you see anything going on. I can't begin to tell you how much fun I'm going to have with all of this."

The end? Not quite yet. A friend and fellow youth leader was a secretary for our local police department. I called her on Monday and mentioned that she would be seeing a report come across her desk with my name and address on it. Any chance she could get me a copy?

"I'll see what I can do," she answered.

A few days later the report showed up in our mailbox. We kept it for the remaining two years that Jon and John were a part of our youth group. And, of course, I made them aware that I possessed a copy. They were both great guys and we thoroughly enjoyed their time in youth group. But, still, it was fun to remind them of all the paperwork from that night: theirs that lasted only briefly and mine, which was filed in a safe place.

When they graduated from high school, Luanne and I were invited to their graduation open houses. Inside the congratulatory cards we gave them was, of course, our copy of the police report. Kind of our way, I guess, of letting them know that things were wiped clean between us.

Chapter 16

BIG SCREEN DEBUT

Among the behaviors we discourage at our youth center is inappropriate contact between the sexes. Given that we have a building full of teenagers it should be no surprise, however, that there are times when hormones trump brain cells.

One evening our staff had to intervene several times between a young man and young woman intent upon physically displaying their affection for one another. After giving them a last warning, our staff continued to keep their eyes on them, especially when the young couple walked into one of our theater rooms. One of our Persons In Charge happened to be near our security booth at the time and, along with our audio-visual tech for the evening, took a quick look at our security camera footage to make sure everything was okay in the theater. It was not.

The screen showed our 31-seat theater with only three people inside, all of them sitting in the front row. In the row from left to right were the girl, her boyfriend, and a male friend who accompanied them into the theater. The couple were locked in a passionate embrace while their friend was enjoying whatever movie that was showing on our four-and-a-half foot high by nine-foot-wide high-definition screen.

"Not again," our PIC, Jamie, said to Nate, the AV tech.

"Yup, afraid so," said Nate.

All I Said Was #*%$

How prevalent is inappropriate behavior inside a community youth center serving a 40-mile radius, multiple school districts, and welcoming several thousand kids a month through our doors? We deal with poor decisions, but it happens way less than you may think. For one thing, we've established very clear expectations when it comes to behavior and we don't waver from those guidelines. Second, kids have bought into the idea that we're a safe sanctuary from much of the junk they deal with on a daily basis. As a result, they're invested in what goes on here and not only tend to act responsibly and respectfully, but they also help us when they see things that need to be addressed. But do we have to deal with occasional knuckleheaded behavior? Sure. And I'm often asked why we choose to put ourselves in a position to have to do so.

There are several answers to that question. First, I was a pretty knuckleheaded kid when I was that age. It gives me patience when I deal with the kind of stuff I would have been doing if I'd had a place like this to hang out in when I was that age.

Second, we're convinced that what we're doing is absolutely, vitally, existentially critical. Allow me to share some truly frightening statistics:

- Suicide rates among adolescents between the ages of 10 to 24 increased 57.4% between 2007 and 2018 (United States Centers for Disease Control and Prevention, National Vital Statistics Report, Volume 69, Number 11, September 11, 2020).
- Suicide rates for children aged 10-14 nearly tripled from 2007 to 2018 (United States Centers for Disease Control and Prevention).
- Suicide is now the second-leading cause of death among adolescents (United States Centers for Disease Control and Prevention).

Kids are suffering. Although there is no universal agreement among mental health professionals regarding the root cause of these alarming statistics, studies are beginning to show links between screen time and social media use and increases in anxiety, depression, and suicide. In a study by experts from San Diego State University and Florida State University published by the Association for Psychological Science, researchers linked screen time and social media use to depressive symptoms and suicide-related outcomes. Specifically, they reported that "adolescents who spent more time on new media (including social media and electronic devices such as smartphones) were more likely to report mental health issues, and adolescents who spent more time on non-screen activities (in-person social interaction, sports/exercise, homework, print media, attending religious services) were less likely." This study also found that teens who use their smartphones more than five hours a day are 70 percent more likely to have suicidal thoughts or actions than those who reported one hour of daily use.

I'm no psychologist. And I understand that there are rarely black and white answers to any particular crisis. Links between increasing adolescent mental health issues and the ubiquitous nature of smartphones and social media may still be anecdotal. But I hang out with kids on a weekly basis. And I can tell you that the overwhelming majority of issues for which kids seek our help have to do with social media. Bullying has gone viral. Technology limits social interaction. Sleep is interrupted by the constant ping of smartphones. And kids perceive their lives as comparing poorly to those they see lived out on social media. It's no surprise that this generation of young people is struggling with feelings of isolation, anger, confusion, and hopelessness. The importance of providing a place where kids can be part of a positive community and where they can experience God's love is more critical than ever.

Finally, we've got such great news that we can't help but share it. We have a sign hanging in our lobby that quotes 1 Thessalonians chapter 2, verse 8: "We love you so much that we shared with you not only God's good news, but our own lives too." To a generation of kids who visit our youth center, we get to be a shining light amidst the darkness. Our prayer continues to be that kids leave our building thinking, "I'm not sure why that place feels different, but I'd sure like to find out why."

All I Said Was #*%$

All this makes the challenge of having to deal with a couple of kids intent upon finding a place to make out seem pretty inconsequential. Still, we have a responsibility. Frustrated, Jamie spent a few seconds looking around our high-tech AV and security booth as he contemplated what to do about the two kids in our movie theater. "Wait a minute," he said to Nate. "We can take any video source in this building and feed it to any screen we want, right?"

"We can," Nate replied.

"Even our security footage?" asked Jamie

"Even our security footage." A grin crossed Nate's face as he realized where this was going.

"Nate," said Jamie, "can you please switch this security camera footage to the screen in the movie theater?"

"Done," said Nate, already having anticipated Jamie's request. They continued to watch the security footage as a new scene unfolded in the theater. I wish had kept the recording of what happened as the movie the three were watching was replaced with footage of the young couple making out—in all its larger-than-life, high-definition glory.

Although they continued to be oblivious to everything except each other, their buddy was not. It took him a few seconds to register what was now showing on the screen. But when he figured it out he almost fell out of his seat, laughing hysterically. He elbowed his buddy, who was obviously none too thrilled to be interrupted. On the silent security feed you could see the buddy point to the screen, still laughing, as his friend turned to look. At that point, two sets of eyes got very large as the culprits realized that not only were they busted, but that their exploits were being broadcast before them larger than life. Having already been warned several times, the two of them sprang from their seats and made a beeline through our building and out the front door, doing their very best to avoid being confronted by any of our staff.

Now, we're not in the business of embarrassing kids. If we were, we'd have broadcast our little soap opera on all 36 screens in our facility as an object lesson to everyone in attendance. However, after having been talked to several times, we decided to try a creative approach. And, we discovered, these kids were visual learners.

The lesson took. The young couple continued to be regular visitors and I can happily report that they became model citizens. Jamie and Nate got the weekly gold star for creative problem solving. And a chapter in this book.

Chapter 17

Eternal Flame

It began in Atlanta in the year 2000. No, not the Olympics. Those were in 1996. Although this competition involves a flame, too.

We were on a church mission trip with our senior high youth group, serving at the Pine Street Shelter in downtown Atlanta. I'm not sure how the conversation started, but somehow during one of those late night, laying on our cots, waiting for everyone to finally be quiet and go to sleep times, the guys asked me about my college years. And somehow the talk got around to my college roommate and how he liked to entertain the guys in our dorm by, well, lighting his flatulence. Can I use the word fart here? OK. He lit his farts. To the extreme amusement of all. It never got old. I mentioned in an earlier chapter that all guys have a junior high part of their brain that never develops beyond that stage, right?

Of course, the high school-aged guys I was bunking with were instantly intrigued.

"That really works?" they asked.

"Of course," I answered. "It's just methane. The most natural of natural gasses."

"No way," they responded. "It's an urban myth, like cow-tipping."

Cow-tipping should be referred to as a rural myth, I thought to myself. But that's beside the point.

"It works, guys, trust me," I answered instead.

"Can we try it?" they asked. Like I couldn't have anticipated that this was where things were headed?

"We'll talk about it," I said. "Let's get some sleep, okay?"

At breakfast the next morning I talked to one of the other adult leaders—obviously I'm using the word adult loosely—about our conversation the previous evening.

"I think we ought to let them try it," he said. "I'll pick up a couple of lighters for tonight."

So what followed wasn't entirely my fault. Thanks, Tim.

After a long day of serving in the shelter and the surrounding streets of Atlanta, it was time to head to our sleeping area. The anticipation among our guys had been palpable all day. They were chomping at the bit to give it a shot. And, I found out later, they had been chomping on cans of pork and beans all day long as well. You've never seen a group of high school guys on a mission trip so eager for bedtime. After setting a few ground rules, we handed over the lighters and, well, waited. Until one of the guys shouted for the lighter, assumed the position, and produced a bright blue flame.

You could have heard the laughter in Macon.

Thus ensued an hour or so of handing around the lighter and exploding in laughter every time someone, well, exploded.

I'm not sure who suggested it, but I'm going to claim it wasn't me. "We ought to have a competition," a voice proposed. Again, I'm blaming it on Tim.

And so it began, in Atlanta, in the year 2000. Our youth group's annual Eternal Flame contest. Held during the last night of each annual mission trip. We even made a trophy—a handheld butane torch inscribed with the name of each year's winner. Over the years, contests were held across the United States in Atlanta, Philadelphia, Nashville, Oklahoma City and rural Kentucky. We even came up with a scoring system that included things like height, duration, volume, color, and an automatic disqualification if something happened to douse the flame. Go ahead. Think about it.

Word, of course, got back to our church board. I was never called before them to explain myself, but I heard that it came up. I can only speculate as to why I wasn't confronted, but our board at the time was all men. Men. Junior high brain. I think they understood.

On the first day of a week-long trip with our group to rural Kentucky after the competition was several years old, I was approached by the two young men running the site for the mission organization. They both appeared a bit hesitant as they walked up to me, leading me to wonder what was up.

"Hey Stan, got a second?" they asked.

"Sure guys," I said. "What's up?"

"Well, we've heard you guys hold an annual competition."

Six hundred miles from home. Two guys I'd never met. How in the world could they know? And now I'm about to be chastised. Scolded. Maybe even confronted about my spiritual condition. Certainly told that we wouldn't be holding our competition that year.

"We were wondering," one of them began.

"Yes?" I answered.

"Well," the other finished. "We were wondering if we could watch."

"Of course!" I was relieved that I wouldn't have to disappoint the boys by calling off that year's competition. And, frankly, thankful that my worthiness as a youth leader wasn't being called into question. At least not by them. "Participate if you'd like!" I offered. And watch they did, laughing as hard as the rest of us as Andy won that year's contest.

A spiritually edifying activity? No. A profound teaching opportunity? Nope. Something that my mom would approve of? Definitely, absolutely, 100% not. Then why, you might ask. Believe me, you wouldn't be the first.

I think it gets back to that idea of authenticity. Of breaking down barriers. And I firmly believe that it allowed me to jump start relationships with guys who might have had inaccurate preconceived notions about followers of Christ. And if our contest swayed even a couple of guys over the years who were on the fence about joining us on one of our trips, then it was worth it.

Chapter 18

Taking Out the Trash

We ran our Kids' Camp for more than fifteen years and found it to be one of the most powerful ministries in which we engaged. Each year we chose a different theme for our teaching, but always during the last evening of each session, we would present the Gospel and invite kids to accept Christ as their Lord and Savior.

During one such session we had the opportunity to celebrate what happens when someone encounters the life-changing power of God for the first time. A young lady who was not a member of our church family—I'll call her Sophie—asked one of our camp counselors to pray with her after the meeting and invited Jesus into her life. Sophie was exhilarated and was crying and laughing all at the same time, which led everyone at camp to join in her celebration. I've rarely had the opportunity to experience such unbridled joy.

After things calmed down a bit, I took Sophie aside and asked her if she'd share her experience in front of our entire congregation the following Sunday. Our youth were invited to lead worship after each Kids' Camp and I knew that Sophie's story would lead to yet another round of celebration when our congregation heard the story.

"I'd be happy to do that," said Sophie. "But I've got a big problem."

"What's that?" I asked.

"I'm Catholic," Sophie replied. "I have no idea how I'm going to tell my mom that I accepted Jesus at a Protestant church camp."

I spent some time reassuring Sophie and asked if there was anything I could do to help, but she said it was her responsibility to talk to her mom. I respected her need to address things on her own, so we rejoined the celebration. It was an incredible evening!

I'm not naïve. I recognize that there are significant differences in theology between Catholic and Protestant traditions. But I also recall a youth meeting I put together that featured our pastor and the priest of the local Catholic parish. We had a number of local Catholic kids who attended our youth group and both they and the kids from our church were asking me questions I couldn't answer. I thought the best solution was to hold a fireside chat where kids could ask Pastor Rod and Father John honest questions and receive expert answers.

I still remember the way Father John opened the meeting. He put a copy of the Apostles' Creed on the screen behind him and said to the Protestant kids in the room, "You all recognize this, right?" We recite the creed regularly during our worship services and, in fact, most of the kids whose families were members of our church were able to recite it by memory.

"Did you know," continued Father John, "that we Catholics pray the Apostles' Creed as a part of our rosary? Let's read it together." So we did:

> I believe in God, the Father almighty,
> creator of heaven and earth.
> I believe in Jesus Christ, his only Son, our Lord.
> He was conceived by the power of the Holy Spirit
> and born of the Virgin Mary.
> He suffered under Pontius Pilate,
> was crucified, died, and was buried.
> He descended to the dead.
> On the third day he rose again.
> He ascended into heaven,

and is seated at the right hand of the Father.
He will come again to judge the living and the dead.
I believe in the Holy Spirit,
the holy catholic Church,
the communion of saints,
the forgiveness of sins,
the resurrection of the body,
and the life everlasting. Amen.

When we were done, Father John asked, "If we agree on this, it makes what we disagree on seem a little less consequential, don't you think?"

As I've said before, I'm no theologian. I recognize that we disagree on some pretty significant issues. But this was the conversation that colored my thought process as I considered the "problem" of a Catholic kid accepting Christ at a Protestant camp. We often tend to complicate things in a way that creates barriers between us. As for me, I know that my job is to love God and love others. I'll leave the rest to someone else.

The following Sunday our group led worship and Sophie's story was the highlight of the morning. She did a phenomenal job relating her experience and, just like at camp, there were few dry eyes in our congregation.

After the service I made a beeline to Sophie to tell her what a blessing her story was to our congregation. "How did your conversation go with your mom?" I asked.

"I haven't had it yet," she replied.

Surprised, I asked her when she planned on talking to her mom.

"Right now," she answered. "When I looked up during my talk I noticed she was in the back row." Sophie looked across our church commons toward a woman standing by herself near the entrance.

Gulp.

"Want me to come along?" I asked.

"Nope," Sophie said. "I should have done this last week."

I watched the conversation from a distance. There were more tears, plus some laughter and, finally, hugs. After a few minutes I walked over to join them and introduced myself to Sophie's mom.

"I'm sorry about all this," I said. "We definitely could have handled things better."

"No need to apologize," she answered. "I don't care if Sophie found Jesus at a Protestant church camp or taking out the trash, what matters is that she's found Jesus!"

Wait. What? Did she just equate our church with carrying garbage to the curb?

It's OK. I knew what she meant. And without her realizing it, the analogy was fantastic. Accepting Christ means taking out the trash, not only initially, but every day after that. I might use that someday, I thought to myself.

Chapter 19

PRAYER NINJAS

It was a little over eight years since we had opened the doors of our community youth center and we were feeling as though it was time to refresh things. We had 5,000 square feet of our facility dedicated to an activity that wasn't as popular as it once was and we thought we could make better use of that area, while adding to the excitement we offered our visitors. I sat down with my co-founder and board president, Joel, and, after a brief discussion about how to proceed, we agreed to do what we'd done from the day we began this journey: pray, asking God what was next and not moving forward until he made it clear. As people of faith, we believe that God has a plan and that it's our responsibility to discern it. This approach had worked for us from the beginning of our journey and we agreed to wait upon God's leading for whatever was next. However long that took.

Our initial decision to make a change took place in mid-February. Over the next several weeks Joel and I prayed individually, waiting for God reveal His plan. Sometime in mid-March I was in the shower, not really thinking about our ministry, when I was struck by an idea for the space: ninja warrior course. Keep in mind that I had never watched the popular television show and really knew nothing about the ninja movement. But there it was. Ninja. And the more I thought about it, the more it fit with what our ministry was about—physical activities that rewarded effort, fearlessness, and persistence. But I had no idea where to start. So I continued to pray, seeking guidance and wisdom.

That revelation took place on a Sunday. Two days later I was in my accountant's office, going over my annual tax return. My accountant, Denny, is familiar with our youth center and mentioned that he had heard that we were in the process of an update. "Got any idea what's next?" he asked.

"I didn't until last weekend," I replied. "But I think God is directing us toward a ninja warrior course."

"Funny you should say that," he said with a hint of a smile. "I happen to have a client who builds ninja courses."

Feeling the goosebumps start to rise, I asked, "Can you give me his contact information?"

"I'll check to see if he's ok with me passing it along," Denny answered.

I signed a few papers and went on my way, looking forward to where this was all going.

Denny got back to me two days later. "I got permission to pass along contact information. I really wanted to say something last week when we met, but you're not going to believe this." He then gave me the name of an old friend named Dan who I hadn't seen in quite a few years. Dan and I had worked together for several years a couple of decades earlier. And now he was in the business of building Ninja courses—not 15 miles from the location of our youth center.

I immediately called Dan and told him what was going on. He was as amazed as I was over the direction of events. After catching up a bit we agreed to meet in four days—just 8 days after my initial shower brainstorm.

Since all of this had happened quite quickly, I hadn't had an opportunity to keep Joel in the loop. Knowing he was on vacation in Florida, I sent him a quick text on Saturday of the same week: "I'm not sure where this is going, but God has been leading me somewhere. I have an appointment set up for Monday and I'll tell you more after my meeting."

After a few minutes my phone chirped. Joel was responding: "Sounds great. Can't wait to hear about it. For what it's worth, I've been thinking ninja."

I almost dropped my phone. The word flabbergasted does not begin to do justice to how I felt. It was one of those rare, pure moments during which there can be no doubt that you're hearing directly from God.

"OH." I texted.

"MY." I typed and hit send.

"WORD." I pushed send again.

"What?!?" he responded.

"My meeting on Monday is with a company that builds ninja courses."

"I guess we know where we're headed," he answered. "Talk to you next week!"

I don't profess to understand why sometimes God makes His plans abundantly clear and other times we need to plead for guidance. Henry Blackaby, in his book *Experiencing God*, has said that, "God speaks by the Holy Spirit through the Bible, prayer, circumstances, and the church to reveal Himself, His purposes, and His ways." That's an approach to discerning God's will that has worked for me. Even then, there are times I wish God would just call me on the phone and tell me what to do. If it were that easy, though, there'd be no faith required. But I will say this: I'm sharp enough to know when He's hitting me over the head with a two-by-four. And this was clearly one of those times. The rest, as they say, is history. By the first of July we had a course designed and built and it's been a huge hit with our visitors. Stealth may be an essential skill for a ninja. But isn't it great when God chooses to make his plans abundantly and undeniably clear?

Chapter 20

An Uplifting Experience

It was mid-January, meaning it was time for our annual youth group snow skiing trip. My wife and I are not great skiers, but we had a passion for teaching young people to ski. Learning to ski tends to be passed on through families and, as a result, some young people never learn because it's not something their families do. As people who learned later in life ourselves, and given the popularity of snow skiing in Michigan, we simply felt that young people ought to be exposed to the sport and given the opportunity to decide if it's something they want to pursue further.

Our approach was always the same: get the kids geared up, spend some time on flat ground helping them understand the basics, and then take them to the bunny hill to show them the fundamentals of turning, stopping and, hopefully, staying upright. Ultimately, once they got their feet under them (literally), our goal was always to get them on a beginner slope so they could experience the thrill of carving their way down the hill.

The biggest obstacle for first-time skiers, however, was not the idea of pointing their skis downhill and trusting their training. Rather, it was the chairlift. To a novice skier there is nothing more intimidating than trying to figure out how to manage this alien-looking, high-speed apparatus designed to scoop you up, transport you above the treetops, and sling you back down to earth at the top of the hill. Despite our best efforts to talk our group of fledgling skiers through the process prior to getting them in line, there was always high anxiety among our kids as we moved ever-closer to our turn to climb aboard.

Normally our approach was to pair Luanne up with a kid in the first chair so she could manage the group as they arrived at the top of the hill. I'd ride up with a kid in the last chair to make sure that everyone got aboard. We'd then ski down the hill in a group, making sure that everyone made it down safely, and then repeat the process. On this particular trip we had an especially anxious first-timer—we'll call her Ashley—who I knew was going to have trouble with the lift. As a result, I paired up with her, hoping to coach her through the process. Ashley and I took our place in line last among our group and, as our turn approached, I talked her through the process of climbing aboard, offering words of encouragement as we watched the chairs whip around the pulley at the bottom of the hill and scoop up the next riders in line.

When our turn arrived, Ashley did a great job of skiing into the loading zone, preparing for the chair to come up behind us, and sitting down as the chair nudged us from behind. Everything went flawlessly and we were airborne! You could see the stress evaporate from Ashley's face as we enjoyed the scenery from 30 feet above the ground. However, dismounting the lift can be as difficult as getting on and I began talking her through the process we'd need to follow when we arrived at the top of the hill. For those of you who have never skied, the chair approaches a ramp where you allow your skies to come into contact with the snow. When you reach the ramp you simply put your skis down, stand up, and ski down the ramp so the chair can clear you and swing around the uphill pulley. The trick, of course, is to not cross the path of your chair partner as you ski down the ramp. If you do, you tend to end up in a tangled heap on the dismount ramp, requiring the lift operator to shut down the lift until you can extricate yourselves from each other's equipment and clear the ramp.

You can see where this is going. We got to the top of our first ride, Ashley got her skis on the ground, stood up ... and promptly skied directly in front of me and took us both out. The lift shut down, we disentangled ourselves, got back to our feet, and then joined our group—who had somewhat gleefully watched the entire scene unfold. It was no big deal, though. It happens. The good news was that we got our group together, pointed them downhill, and celebrated as everyone successfully navigated their first-ever trip down a ski hill!

We made our way back to the lift and prepared for our ride back up the hill. The tension was much less palpable as we got in line, Luanne once again leading the way and me bringing up the rear with Ashley. We mounted the lift without a hitch, enjoyed the ride and, at the top, Ashley once again skied across my path and took us both out. Lift shuts down, we got off the ground, kids giggled, and we skied back down the hill.

This happened yet again on our third trip up the hill. I could tell that the lift operator was getting frustrated, as was Ashley. Remembering that someone once defined insanity as doing the same thing over and over again expecting a different result, I hatched a new plan for our fourth trip. I figured I'd let Ashley dismount first and ski down the ramp and I'd wait until the last possible second to jump off the chair and then follow her down the ramp. An OK idea in theory.

We reached the unloading area. Ashley got off first, which worked perfectly. She stood up and skied down the ramp without incident. I, however, waited too long to get out of the chair: it hooked an open pocket on my jacket and began its slingshot move around the uphill pulley, flinging me to the ground at high speed from about six feet in the air.

The impact with the ground knocked the wind out of me and, I found out early the next week, cracked one of my ribs. I remained still, face-first on the ground, trying to regain my breath—which was not an encouraging sight for the crowd of onlookers or the lift operator. In fact, near-panic ensued as our group—and especially Luanne—made their way to me in an effort to ascertain how badly I was damaged. A couple members of the ski patrol appeared as well, mumbling something under their breath about the lift being a one-way ride.

Thomas Edison is credited with having said, after being questioned about his many missteps as he struggled to invent a working lightbulb, "I have not failed 10,000 times—I've successfully found 10,000 ways that will not work." Winston Churchill said, "Success is stumbling from failure to failure with no loss of enthusiasm." I heartily agree with both sentiments. Fear of failure paralyzes us, especially in a culture that seems intent upon pointing out and celebrating our miscues. In fact, snow skiing is a great allegory for this truth. Whenever I see someone on the ski hill who doesn't display the effects of taking a few spills, my first thought is that they're not trying very hard. Cruising through life trying to avoid bumps and bruises doesn't result in much growth. Not impressed with Edison or Churchill's thoughts on failure? Then how about this quote: "The greatest teacher, failure is." It's hard to argue with the wisdom of Yoda.

There is a risk that fearlessness can be viewed as arrogance. It's happened to me. I'd really, *really* like to think that's a misunderstanding by people who don't know me. It's not that I think I'm always right. It's just that I'm not afraid of being wrong.

This quote by Theodore Roosevelt eloquently sums up this topic:

> "It is not the critic who counts; not the man who points out how the strong man stumbles, or where the doer of deeds could have done them better. The credit belongs to the man who is actually in the arena, whose face is marred by dust and sweat and blood; who strives valiantly; who errs, who comes short again and again . . . and who, at the worst, if he fails, at least fails while daring greatly, so that his place shall never be with those cold and timid souls who neither know victory nor defeat."

The most ubiquitous command in all of scripture is "Fear not!" Take that to heart. To borrow from Allstate, remember that you're in good hands.

An Uplifting Experience

Back to my epic ski lift failure. Within a couple of minutes I had caught my breath and made it back to my feet. In fact, I was able to spend the remainder of the day on the hill with our group, albeit a bit hunched over and breathless from the pain in my ribs. Someone else also took over riding the lift with Ashley but, I can happily report, she figured things out and rode the rest of the afternoon without incident.

If there are "be-on-the-lookout-for" posters in ski lift operator shacks, I suspect my face is posted at that particular resort. As well as a notation in my medical records describing a particularly unique way to break one's ribs while skiing. But at the end of the day we were able to celebrate with a group of kids who overcame their fears and who got back up more times than they fell down. That's always worth celebrating.

Chapter 21

DIVE! DIVE! DIVE!

Each fall we held a weekend retreat for our junior high and senior high youth staff from our church. We'd find a camp or lake to hang out at and spend Friday evening through Sunday afternoon worshipping together, planning our ministry year, eating great food, and having a lot of fun.

On this particular trip we were staying at a home on a beautiful inland lake an hour or so from home. On Friday evening we decided to enjoy a nighttime cruise around the lake on the pontoon boat at our disposal. We loaded twenty of us onto a boat designed to hold twelve and took off on a leisurely voyage across the almost glass-like water.

I'm not much of a swimmer. I didn't grow up swimming and only learned the fundamentals at a YMCA class for adults in my mid-thirties. Although I had completed that class by this time, I was still extremely uncomfortable around water over my head.

One of our male junior high leaders was at the helm while the rest of us lounged in other parts of the boat, including three of our female junior high leaders at the bow with their feet dangling in the warm water. My wife and I sat on a comfortable bench underneath a canopy at the back of the boat, enjoying the warm air, great fellowship, and the twinkling lights of cottages on the shore.

Dive! Dive! Dive!

Halfway into our voyage one of the women on the front of the boat asked if she could try her hand at driving. She got up from the bow and walked to the helm where our pilot, a former high school football player who weighed at least 250 pounds, gave her a brief tutorial. After she felt comfortable, our male leader walked to her former position on the bow and, for fun, dropped his entire bulk into her spot on the front of the boat. At the same exact time, our novice driver shoved the throttle all the way forward, pushing the boat to full acceleration.

The result of these simultaneous actions caused the boat to begin to dive toward the bottom of the lake like a submarine. Water washed up over the deck, adding weight to the craft, amplifying the effect. The lovely calm of the leisurely boat ride was broken by the panic that ensued as we did our best imitation of the Red October – a submarine in full dive mode headed toward the bottom of the lake.

Looking back I know it would require a catastrophic failure of the air-filled pontoons for the boat to actually sink. But in that moment, all I knew was that we were going under. And I was beneath the boat's canopy. Several hundred yards from shore. Calculating in my mind if I had it in me to swim that far. Trying to remember where the lifejackets were stashed.

In the meantime, someone grabbed the throttle and threw the boat into neutral. The boat popped back to the surface like a cork. The entire episode lasted only half-a-dozen seconds, but it was more than enough to get everyone's heart racing for a few minutes afterward.

This experience gave me a new appreciation for Peter's response when Jesus invited him to walk on water. It's easy to read that story and belittle Peter's actions, being safe and dry at our desk or in our recliner rather than on a small wooden boat in the middle of a large lake being buffeted by a fierce wind. Faith is easy . . . well . . . when it's easy. It's the times when you're headed for the bottom when it's tested. Those times can at best be unpleasant and at worst terrifying. Demoralizing. Faith-shaking. It's the image of Jesus reaching out His hand to Peter to save him from drowning that offers us hope during the most difficult of times. That image should give us great confidence as we embark daily upon the often-choppy waters of serving Him.

Chapter 22

LAS LUCES AZULES

It was a Friday evening at our community youth center. Closing time had come and gone and I found myself sitting in my office at 11pm with four boys whose ride home had not yet arrived. The boys were sheepish and embarrassed that several hundred young people had already been picked up but nobody had arrived to take them home. They were polite yet unwilling to engage me as they spoke amongst themselves in Spanish and made numerous phone calls to parents, grandparents, siblings, neighbors, and anyone else who might be able to come and get them.

Fifteen minutes elapsed. Then thirty. Forty-five minutes went by, as did an hour, as they continued to try to find someone who would answer the phone or who was available to give them a ride. They would answer my questions in English as I checked on their progress while catching up on some correspondence and paperwork at my desk, but only with brief answers and mostly downcast eyes.

As much as I would have liked to give them a ride, in large part so that I could head home after a very long day, our policy is not to do so. First, it puts our staff at risk from a number of different standpoints. Second, if word got out that we provided rides home we'd soon be providing rides for hundreds of kids every night. Lastly, I had driven my pick-up that evening and simply didn't have room for them all.

Finally, after an hour and a quarter of trying and after each of them made several attempts, one of the boys reached an aunt who was available to provide a ride. Again, in Spanish, the young man who had found someone to pick them up provided directions to his *tia* on how to find our building. In the course of his description I heard him use the phrase *las luces azules* to provide a landmark.

After he hung up and shared the good news with his friends, he looked at me and told me, again in English, that his aunt was on her way.

"You told her to look for the blue lights," I responded. "That was a good idea." Our building has programmable show lights on the exterior that were running a blue theme that evening—*las luces azules*.

"Yeah," he said. "She hasn't been here before so I thought that would—" Suddenly his eyes got reaaallllly big as he stopped in mid-reply, realizing that I had understood his phone conversation. Then his eyes shifted back and forth in a panic as, I suspect, he ran every conversation over in his mind that he and his friends had had over the previous hour or so, now realizing that I might have understood.

"You speak Spanish?" he asked, more than a bit panicked.

At this, every other set of eyes in my office locked onto mine, performing, I suspect, the same mental calculus, trying to remember if they'd said anything that might get them into trouble.

"Some." I enjoyed the sense of alarm that was now playing out before my eyes without letting it show too much.

"How did you learn?" one of the boys asked after concluding that they had been more than polite and appropriate during their time in my office.

We then proceeded to have a great conversation about my growing up on a West Michigan apple orchard and the need to learn Spanish in that environment, of my two years of college Spanish classes, and of my time as a construction site manager and the importance of being able to communicate with work crews who spoke primarily Spanish. We laughed about my terrible pronunciation and they tested me a bit to see what I really understood. I was able to adequately hide the fact that I understood way less than I let on and that, truthfully, I speak Spanish *como un nino de tres anos*—like a three-year-old child. We've found, however, that as adults operating a youth center it's best that kids think we're more aware than we actually are. *Lo siento.* Please forgive me for my deceit.

At a time in our history when there seems to be far more shouting than listening, this experience was a powerful reminder for me of the importance of keeping my mouth shut. Granted, there wasn't much I could have added to the conversation in Spanish so I can't say I made a conscious decision to sit at my desk and do my best to understand what was going on around me. But I am thankful that I was forced to exercise my ears and simply take in what was being said. As someone who far too often falls in love with the sound of his own voice, this act of listening provided me with a means of engaging with these young men that likely wouldn't have happened had I been dominating the conversation.

And here's the real challenge: those of us in leadership positions have come to believe that it's our job to talk the most. That we lead people by leading the conversation. This experience reminded me that the best leaders listen more than they talk. God has to re-teach me this lesson fairly regularly. The Greek philosopher Diogenes, who lived in the 300s BCE, put it this way: "We have two ears and one tongue so that we would listen more and talk less."

Our conversation continued as we waited for their ride. I asked about what schools they attended, what they liked to do for fun, how they enjoyed our ministry, and a host of other things. Their hesitancy and reluctance disappeared and we spent a few minutes getting to know each other before we saw headlights in the parking lot. They apologized for keeping me, thanked me for staying, and were on their way.

From that point forward, as they continued to visit us on weekends, and as we ran into each other in our facility, we'd greet each other and they'd test my Spanish or try to teach me some

All I Said Was #*%$

new phrases, always with a smile on our faces. The barriers that had existed early in our time in my office had evaporated and we developed a relationship that would not have existed had it not been for our wait for their ride—and those *luces azules*. A true blue-light special.

Chapter 23

JOKING AROUND

During the time I was involved in church youth ministry I was blessed to be part of a senior high leadership team that remained intact—except for the need to add more adult leaders as the ministry grew—for almost 18 years. This was a group of people who loved Jesus, loved kids, and was extraordinarily dedicated to sharing God's love with the hundreds and hundreds of kids God brought to us over the years. Being part of a group like this, of one mind and spirit, is a rare thing and we treasured all the ways God was at work among us and through us.

We loved each other deeply and often expressed that love by pranking each other mercilessly. It was always good-natured fun, and it was one way in which we expressed how much we cared for each other. Usually, anyway.

We were on one of our annual summer mission trips, this time in Nashville, Tennessee. As always, we split the kids up into work groups, led by two adults per team. For whatever reason, the pranks between adults started earlier than normal during this trip and escalated quickly. After a morning when one group found the tires on their van minus air and an evening when one work team coated another's van with raw eggs and flour, I realized it was time to have a talk with our adult team about our behavior before things got out of hand and someone's feelings were hurt. Plus, we weren't being very good examples to our kids.

There's a reason there are bookshelves full of leadership manuals: leadership is not for the faint of heart. And it's *way* more art than science, especially when it comes to guiding the behavior of others. Fortunately, Scripture provides us with some excellent guidance. Consider Matthew 18:15-17a:

> "If your brother sins against you, go and tell him his fault, between you and him alone. If he listens to you, you have gained your brother. But if he does not listen, take one or two others along with you, that every charge may be established by the evidence of two or three witnesses. If he refuses to listen to them, tell it to the church."

Likewise, the Bible is clear about gossip—defined as unconstrained conversation about other people. In Romans 1:29-30, the Apostle Paul equates gossip with, among other things, evil, malice, envy, murder, slander, and hatred toward God. Did you catch that? Gossip is as bad as murder and hatred toward God.

When we're correcting those we lead this means we do so one-on-one rather than involving others in the conversation. It means we avoid complaining about them to someone else. Despite how difficult it can often be, it means loving others enough to be willing to sit down with them and try to figure out how we can better fulfill God's call upon our lives. Gossip is poison and it's a favorite tool of Satan when he wants to destroy a team of people intent upon furthering God's Kingdom. The ability to lead is vitally dependent upon trust. People won't follow someone they don't trust. And folks won't trust someone who is talking about them behind their backs.

I've been occasionally criticized for this approach. Not because I'm doing things wrong but because it sometimes appears as though I'm doing nothing at all. Members of the team see another team member who may need some guidance and wonder why I'm not addressing the issue. Because I'm doing so privately and because I won't discuss one team member with another, they have no way of knowing the amount of time I may be investing in any particular team member. Another price of leadership.

I collect quotes. In fact, the bulletin board next to my desk is plastered with dozens of pithy sayings and wise words that have struck me in some fashion over the years. These quotes summarize and clarify particular truths with an eloquence to which I can only aspire. Among my very favorites is one by Eleanor Roosevelt: "Great minds discuss ideas. Average minds discuss events. Small minds discuss people."

Amen to that.

Back to our prank war in Nashville. I had a few conversations with our adult team about their behavior. I don't remember who I met with or what I said and, frankly, the number of times I needed to do this with this particular team over our 18 years together could probably be counted on one hand. But I do know the conversations were honest, loving, and resulted in a suspension of hostilities.

In fact, during our leaders meeting that evening Joel reported on his team's activities that day, including a story about an opportunity they had to help a stranger. Apparently, when they arrived at their work site—a local daycare—they encountered a pregnant woman who had just dropped off her child and was headed to a very important job interview. Unfortunately, her tire had gone flat while she was inside and she was beside herself, looking at the tire and coming to terms with the fact that she was going to miss her appointment.

Joel grabbed my son, Andrew, who was a part of the work team, and started to problem-solve. Joel and Andrew quickly pulled the flat tire off her car, threw it in our church van, drove the lady to her job interview, dropped her off, and then drove to a tire shop to get the flat repaired.

After waiting for the repair, Joel and Andrew drove back to the daycare, replaced the tire, and then Joel drove the lady's car back to her interview location, instructing Andrew to follow him in our church van. Dutifully following instructions, Andrew jumped in the driver's seat, started the van, and tailed Joel so that the two of them could ultimately rejoin their team at the daycare. Whew.

At the end of his story, Joel happily reported that not only had he resisted any practical jokes that day, but that they had likely saved this woman's opportunity to be considered for a job she desperately needed.

"You did what?!?" I asked.

Joel, surprised a bit at my tone, looked confused.

"Andrew and I helped a pregnant lady get to her job interview," he said, thinking I'd be happy to hear that he involved my son in the good deed.

"Joel," I said. "Andrew is fifteen years old. He doesn't have his drivers' license yet."

Joel was crestfallen. "Even on a day when I thought I finally did everything right, I screwed up." The group burst into laughter at Joel's chagrin.

Another of our team leaders, Julie, had suffered the entire week in the July heat with the one van in our group lacking air conditioning. Even though she didn't complain, it was clear that she and her group were suffering. Taking pity on Julie, I offered her my van for the last workday of the trip. She gladly accepted and she and her team headed off to their daily work site the next morning with big smiles on their faces.

A few minutes later, as I was driving my group to our site, I got a phone call from Julie.

"Stan," she said. "I'm not sure what I'm doing wrong, but I can't get the air conditioning in this van to work, either. Do you have any suggestions?"

I wonder if it had anything to do with the fact that I had her air conditioner fuse tucked away safely in my pocket. I know, I know. Do as I say, not as I do, right?

Chapter 24

SEARCHING FOR LEADERS

Our senior high youth group held an annual event for a few years that we called our Leader Hunt. Our adult leaders would disguise themselves and then disperse throughout the local mall. We'd bus our kids to the mall and divide them up into teams of five or six. Their challenge was to find as many of their leaders as possible and collect a card from each leader they found. The team of kids with the most cards after an hour and a half would be declared the winners. We never asked the local mall if it was OK for us to do this. We figured we'd rather ask for forgiveness than permission should the need ever arise.

Committed to excellence as always, our adults went all-out for these events. On this occasion, one of them dressed up in the uniform of a friend who worked for the movie theater in the mall and busied herself cleaning the glass on the theater's entry doors. One leader got permission from a tuxedo shop, dressed up in a tux, and stood among the mannequins in their display window. One of our unmarried leaders borrowed a friend's husband and toddler, dressed up as if she were pregnant, and pushed a stroller with her new "family" throughout the mall. I spent an hour in a chair before the event with a woman from our church who did makeup for a local community theater, letting her add 20 years to my appearance. With powdered hair, pancake makeup, freshly added wrinkles, and a wardrobe bought at the local thrift shop I was able to give my wife a preview of coming attractions. Given her response, it was apparently very realistic. Others among our group of adults donned equally creative disguises, determined to blend in with the crowd and not be found.

Interestingly, some of our leaders asked if they could beg off on this one. That was fine, because we needed some of them to transport the kids and oversee the event itself. But I was curious as to why they were reluctant to participate. Although none of them could easily put their finger on it, I heard words like *uncomfortable*, *conspicuous*, *fake*, and others. Exploring it a bit further in following weeks, it became clear that the fundamental issue was that they felt uneasy pretending to be someone they were not.

After some contemplation, that made perfect sense to me. After all, this was a group of adults who was committed to authenticity—a critical component of our ministry's success. Adults who come across as fake set off this current generation's B.S. meters. Since they were old enough to be plopped in front of a television, someone has been trying to sell them something. Do you doubt that kids are aggressively marketed to? Take a look at the toy shelves of your local department store and check out the action figures on display from movies created for kids. Young people today are hyper aware of inauthenticity and immediately tune out attempts to sell them something—including adults who may be trying too hard to be something they're not.

Not to pick on my wife again, but Luanne is the perfect example of being true to who she is. Youth group activities are, to put it mildly, often high energy. And that is not Luanne's wheelhouse. I would often pick my head up in the middle of some kind of madness and see Lu, not disengaged from what was going on, but half a step outside of the craziness. And always with a group of four or five young people in her immediate vicinity, not quite clinging to her, but almost. These were kids who, like Luanne, were just a bit overwhelmed by the chaos and who sought her calming influence. They were kindred spirits. This was yet another example of the body of Christ working together. While the rest of us were ministering to the kids who thrived on pandemonium, Luanne served the kids who sought something less overwhelming.

This all leads to what might be the best advice I can give to anyone considering a role in youth ministry: be yourself. Kids don't expect you to be great. Just real. Author Rachel Held Evans put it this way:

> "We millennials have been advertised to our entire lives, and we can tell when somebody is just trying to sell us something. I think church is the last place I want to go to be sold another product."

I can attest to the truth of that statement. Inauthenticity is probably the number one cause I've seen over the years for adults who have decided to move on from youth ministry due to feelings of ineffectiveness.

In full disguise, I decided to sit in the food court of the mall, since my height makes it hard to hide in a crowd. But after thirty minutes of not being approached by a single group, I got bored. Getting up, I shuffled away from my table, trying to mimic the posture and gait I had developed watching older people move. I made my way around the walkways of the mall and ended up being found by a couple of groups of kids but, given that we had more than a dozen teams on the lookout, my disguise was obviously effective. Finally, from across the mall I spotted the group I'd been looking for: the one that included my son Andrew. I approached them from the opposite direction, passing by closely enough to almost brush shoulders, but received not a glint of recognition from any of them. It wasn't until I was fifteen or twenty feet past them that I heard my son say, "Wait a minute! I think that was my dad!!" The entire group did a one-eighty, approached me with curious looks, and then burst out laughing as they figured out it was really me. Giving them their card, I moved on, disappearing back into the crowd of shoppers.

This event fizzled out after a few years' time. Not because the kids didn't enjoy it, but because the adults couldn't sustain it. More and more of the team expressed their discomfort with disguising

All I Said Was #*%$

themselves, until we could no longer put together a big enough group to make the event work. I was OK with that. I understood. Pretending to be someone they weren't just wasn't in their skillset.

Chapter 25

BEEP, BEEP!

Each evening before we open our youth center we hold a brief staff meeting to share what's going on in our lives, discuss upcoming events, and touch base on operational or behavioral issues that may need our attention. On this particular evening I brought up an ongoing behavioral issue that I thought we needed to be aware of. At the end of my comments, I said, "We're like Wile E. Coyote chasing the Roadrunner. It feels like the kids are always a step ahead of us."

Blank looks. Every face. All around the circle.

"You know. Beep, Beep?" I offered.

Their looks morphed from confusion to concern, as if I was taking a trip on the crazy train. Like I had gone, you know, Looney Tunes.

"You can't tell me none of you knows the Roadrunner," I almost pleaded. "Surely you can't be serious. Raise your hand if you've at least heard of him."

Not a single hand among the dozen or so twenty-somethings. Inconceivable!

At that moment I arrived at a destination I had been approaching for several years: my cultural references were now completely irrelevant. For someone who loves movies and music and who liberally uses lines and lyrics in my communication, I was devastated. In fact, when Luanne asked me out for our first date, she took me to see *Caddyshack*. Even at that early juncture in our relationship, I knew she was a keeper based solely on that decision. I can still recite Bill Murray's monologue about the Dalai Lama from memory. So I got that going for me. Which is nice.

But I digress. Why does this matter? I believe we use these cultural references as communication shorthand. I can say things like, "we're going to need a bigger boat" or "we're not in Kansas anymore" to my wife and she knows exactly what I'm trying to tell her. Further, these references help to reflect a shared experience and join us to a particular community. They foster a sense of belonging. So in a business in which building relationships is everything, I'm at a distinct disadvantage when I no longer speak the language of the people with whom I'm in relationship.

I once heard someone describe youth ministry as missionary work. We're called to leave what we know to immerse ourselves in another culture. Duffy Robbins put it this way: "Youth ministry is a cross-cultural ministry. It requires people of one culture (adults)—with one set of values and mores regarding fashion, leisure, volume of music, and so on—to cross over into the world of another culture (teenagers) with its distinct language, customs, art, and preferences." As a result, we can't expect young people to understand and respond to our references. We need to become, if not fluent, at least competent in theirs.

There's a huge risk to this. There's a fine line between understanding and pandering. A guy in his fifties trying to sound like a teenager is a pitiful thing. It's the cultural equivalent of reacting to a mid-life crisis by buying a red convertible sports car and driving around with your shirt partially unbuttoned to show off your gold chains. It's embarrassing. Kids see right through it. And, as we said before, they'll tune out insincerity in a New York minute. What we've got here is a failure to communicate, and I wish you all the luck in the world as you try to navigate this minefield. Just remember, all you need is love. May the force be with you.

There are plenty of resources available that explore what it takes to develop cultural intelligence, so I won't try to reproduce all that information here. However, there are a few specific things I've picked up along the way that have helped me relate to people several generations younger than myself:

Understand and be comfortable with who you are. I am well aware that I'm an old Michigan farm boy who loves puns, trivia, Hollywood musicals, the Detroit Tigers, and 70s rock and roll. You won't embarrass me by pointing any of that out. I accepted who I am long ago. Self-awareness serves as an anchor when we enter the stormy seas of the unknown.

Express authentic interest in the individual and their culture. It's easy to generalize about particular groups. Don't make that mistake. As my favorite philosopher Ted Lasso says, be curious, not judgmental.

Find things in common. Regardless of differences in age, there are always things we can find in common. When we establish these kinds of connections, barriers disappear.

Ask questions and listen to answers. As much as we love to talk about ourselves, resist the urge. Other people do as well. Give them that opportunity.

Don't appropriate. Oh my goodness. Please! Is there anything more embarrassing?

Risk making mistakes. Because you will. And it's okay. Apologize. Learn. Move on.

So I try to know a bit about what content kids are currently streaming. The name of the current Bachelor. And I try to keep the music in our facility playlist up-to-date. But I still occasionally drop a reference to Bruce Springsteen or Ferris Bueller. After all, as Popeye says, "I am what I am." Wait, you know who Popeye is, right? Oops, I did it again.

Chapter 26

LEGACY

We employ a small number of part-time paid staff during our youth center's open-to-the-public hours. These staff members fill a variety of roles that supplement the efforts of our volunteers and that require a higher level of training and responsibility than what we expect from those who give of their time. Included in those paid positions are what we call our Persons In Charge, otherwise known as PICs. We always have two PICs in attendance during our community events and their responsibility is exactly as it sounds: they oversee the kids in attendance, guide and direct our volunteers and other paid staff, and interact with parents who have questions or concerns about our ministry. They are highly trained, assume a great deal of responsibility, and free me from having to be at our facility every single hour that we're open. And they are young; most of them are in their early to mid-twenties.

One Friday evening, after we had gotten all the kids through our admission stations and things had settled into their normal evening routine, I caught up with one of our PICs. Kali was a nursing student at the time, so I asked how school was going.

"I just started a new clinical rotation," Kali said. "I'm working in the pediatric ER at the children's hospital."

"Wow." I was truly impressed with her tackling such a challenging assignment and imagining the trauma, chaos, and fear permeating such an environment. "That's gotta be intense!"

"Yeah, it is," she answered. "I couldn't do it if I hadn't worked here first."

That stopped me in my tracks.

"What do you mean?" I asked, but I was pretty sure I already knew what she was talking about.

"Being in charge of this place and dealing with all of the stuff I've had to deal with really prepared me for the pressure and demands of this placement."

Wow.

At this point Kali had been with us for about three years, having progressed through the ranks to become a PIC, and I remember her first few times in our building. As you can imagine, a large youth center filled with several hundred junior-high-aged students on a Friday evening can be a loud, chaotic, and intimidating place. And like many folks who wade into the middle of it, Kali's initial response was what we like to call deer in the headlights—that wide-eyed anticipation that something is about to happen that is going to require you to flee. No matter how much training we provide, there's no way to fully prepare someone for the demands of serving in a place like this and it initially can be a bit overwhelming. I've had this conversation with Kali many times so I'm not speaking out of turn when I say that she had come as far as any staff member we've ever employed when it comes to growing into her role. She had progressed from wondering what in the world she was doing here to projecting a sense of calm and confident awareness of her ability to address whatever this place might throw her way. I always feel a sense of confidence and comfort on the evenings I know she's in charge.

When our team of founders—eight husbands, wives, friends, and co-workers—first began dreaming about this ministry journey we focused exclusively on the impact we hoped to make on the kids who visited us. But, as always, God has a habit of doing more than we ask or imagine. Now that we're more than a decade into this thing, we've come to the conclusion that perhaps the greatest legacy of this ministry will not be the impact we have on our visitors but, rather, on the generation of young people who have stepped into leadership roles here and who have gained experience that will serve them in amazing ways as they move into their full-time careers, next phases of life, or whatever else God has in store for them.

People will tell you that if you want to engage in ministry you need to attend a Bible college, get a degree in youth ministry or theology, work toward your ordination, and find full-time employment at a church. Hogwash (I had another word in mind but I've already written a chapter about profanity so I refrained). No offense to those who have been called to professional ministry, but they can't build God's Kingdom on their own. It takes people who are passionate about sharing Christ's love as they take care of patients, sell shoes, create wedding videos, teach kids, sell real estate, manage human resources, or fight fires—all professions pursued by former or current staff members here. These young folks have overcome their anxiety, gained valuable experience, assumed incredible responsibility, and learned to pursue their passion for sharing the Good News, and they will impact their communities in powerful ways. They will likely be the ultimate legacy of this ministry.

Knowing Kali, she will be uncomfortable that I've singled her out. And, frankly, doing so is unfair to the dozens of other staff members here about whom I could have written a chapter—sorry, guys. But Kali's story is the perfect example of how God can use both a ministry and His people in ways that we never anticipate. That sense of the unknown, of wondering what's next, adds to the adventure of joining God on this journey he's called us to. And the fearlessness of the young people who serve here as they buckle up for whatever is next is a testimony to their faith and obedience.

Chapter 27

GENERATIONS

Do you want to know how to tell you're really getting old? It's not gray hair, or achy joints, or age spots, or having to get up three times a night to pee. It's this: I just spent twenty minutes catching up with a young man who was a part of the youth group I formerly led who—wait for it—just dropped off his fifth-grade daughter at our community youth center for the evening.

Ouch.

French singer Maurice Chavalier famously said, "Old age isn't so bad if you consider the alternative." So don't get me wrong. I'm not grumbling (much) about getting older. But talk about getting hit with a dose of reality. How is it that everyone else seems to be aging so much more quickly than me?

I'm grateful for the privilege of a long career in youth ministry. Unfortunately, longevity in youth ministry is a rare thing. I once heard someone quote a statistic indicating that the average youth pastor lasts about a year-and-a-half in his or her job. I have no data to support that claim and, frankly, I'm not sure how you'd measure it anyway. But I can tell you from practical experience that it doesn't sound that far-fetched. In a world where many kids are searching for any kind of consistency they can find, we seem to have a problem providing it.

All I Said Was #*%$

Why is that? I think there are a couple of obvious reasons. First, youth ministry is often viewed as a stepping-stone to "more important ministry." Too often youth pastors are asked when they plan to move on to an associate or head pastor job, as if that should be the goal of everyone entering ministry. In fact, I've heard stories from youth workers who've had members of their congregations wonder what was wrong with them for wanting to remain in youth ministry, as if it's a lack of initiative or a warped motivation that keeps them from walking away from their calling. Certainly there are folks who do, in fact, view their time in youth ministry as a training ground for leading an entire church. There's nothing wrong with that. But we need to re-think this idea that there's something wrong with people who wish to remain faithful to their calling to invest in kids, and then support them in their obedience.

Second, we're throwing young people stepping into their first ministry jobs to the wolves. We're putting 22-year-olds in positions where everyone in their congregation thinks they could do the job better. Newly minted graduates are not prepared for the demands of working for a church and they haven't, in most cases, developed the thick skin or set of skills needed to navigate the treacherous waters of church politics. So they get interrogated, undermined, and attacked by folks who may not be able to express what they're in favor of but can definitely shout about what they're against. No wonder these young people question their calling and eventually seek a calmer and safer harbor somewhere else.

This is not to say all churches get it wrong. There are many who surround their young hires with a team of wise and experienced people who can run interference, share wisdom, and provide valuable mentorship. But we need to do a better job of both preparing students for the rigors of church ministry and helping congregations understand their responsibility to support, respect, and love the people they've placed in positions of leadership.

So anyway, I'm getting older. But the advantage of age is, at least theoretically, the accumulation of wisdom, experience, patience, and understanding. Although my favorite poet, Ogden

Nash, once said, "You are only young once, but you can stay immature indefinitely." This book may prove his point.

Perhaps the primary disadvantage of getting older is that time seems to speed up. But borrowing one final quote, this one from John D. MacDonald's beloved character Travis McGee: "Today, my friends, we each have one more day, every one of us. And joy is the only thing that slows the clock."

Amen, McGee.

Chapter 28

Not the Last Word

Our church youth group was spending the weekend at a biennial youth conference in Northern Michigan. The featured speaker for the event was Christian sociologist Tony Campolo. As was the typical practice at this event, the speaker hosted a breakfast meeting on Saturday morning for the several hundred adult youth leaders in attendance. At this meeting Campolo opened the floor to questions and a friend of mine, Don, who was a youth leader at another church, stood to ask a question.

"I'm not getting any younger," Don said. "How will I know when it's time to quit youth ministry?"

"You can never quit youth ministry," Campolo replied, a deadly serious look on his face. "If you do, you'll go to hell. Next question?"

Scattered uncomfortable laughter spread across the room as we all waited for Tony to follow up on his statement or somehow let Don off the hook.

"I'm serious," Campolo said. "Next question."

Don sat down and, in a welcomed attempt to relieve the tension in the room, someone else rose to ask a different question. I have no idea what it was. For all I can remember, it might have been for directions to the restroom. Don's question and Dr. Campolo's response took the air out of the room.

This meeting occurred more than 20 years ago and it still sticks with me. It has with Don, too. I know this because he now serves on our youth center's board of directors and, even though his role in youth ministry has changed, he remains committed to making a difference in young people's lives. He took Dr. Campolo's answer to heart.

Of course, those of us who serve in youth ministry can move on, and we know that doing so does not consign us to hell. God can change His call upon our lives as He sees fit. I also don't think Tony Campolo was espousing a works-based theology. Rather, I believe his point was this: investing in the lives of young people is critically important. And we dare not treat our calling to do so lightly.

As for me, I'm convinced that I'm still exactly where God has called me to be. Investing in young people remains absolutely essential to me. Today's digital age makes growing up more difficult than ever. Bullying is viral, technology limits social interaction, and advertising promotes unattainable standards. This, combined with the effects of the recent pandemic, has led to a generation of young people that struggles more than ever with feelings of isolation, confusion, anxiety, anger, and hopelessness. As adults, we have an obligation to build authentic relationships with young people, earning the right to invest in their lives and point to a way of life that includes meaning, hope, and purpose—and, ultimately, Jesus. The fact that God continues to bless me with hilarious, ridiculous, unexpected, and sublime experiences as I follow his will is simply a bonus. If I was the cursing type, I might say that's something worth giving a #*%$ about.

www.ingramcontent.com/pod-product-compliance
Lightning Source LLC
Chambersburg PA
CBHW070302100426
42743CB00011B/2313